United Nations Organisation

-------- Emerging Scenario --------

Dr. S. P. Sharma

Raj Publications

New Delhi-110002 (INDIA)

United Nations Organisation: ---Emerging Scenario---

First Published in 2009

ISBN: 978-81-86208-65-6

Published by : **Raj Publications**
108, 4855/24, Ansari Road
Daryaganj, New Delhi - 110 002
Tel. : 011 - 30120939, 9811010939
E Mail: rajpublications@yahoo.co.in

Laser Typesetting by : Tamalika Computers, Delhi

Printed at : GS Offset Printers, Delhi

PRINTED IN INDIA

United Nations Organisation

-------- Emerging Scenario --------

United Nations Organisation

-------- Emerging Scenario --------

Dr. S. P. Sharma

Raj Publications

New Delhi-110002 (INDIA)

United Nations Organisation: ---Emerging Scenario---

First Published in 2009

ISBN: 978-81-86208-65-6

Published by : **Raj Publications**
108, 4855/24, Ansari Road
Daryaganj, New Delhi - 110 002
Tel. : 011 - 30120939, 9811010939
E Mail: rajpublications@yahoo.co.in

Laser Typesetting by : Tamalika Computers, Delhi

Printed at : GS Offset Printers, Delhi

PRINTED IN INDIA

Contents

Preface

The United Nations plays a singular role in the discussion over the future of international affair. Although founded in 1945 and thus already some six decades old, the organization sometimes gives the impression that it is still in need of a founding. Whether it be peacekeeping, strengthening human rights, dealing with problems of the global environment, or the struggle against international terrorism and its manifold causes, there hardly seems to be a global problem in the world today in which the United Nations is not expected to play a key role. On the other hand, it is always pointed out in the very same breath that, for the UN to play its role adequately, it stands in need of reform and renewal. Moreover, a fundamental change in perspective - especially on the part of the more powerful member states - is necesary for the UN's success.

A further complaint often heard is that on especially important issues - such as the recent war in Iraq - the UN is frequently avoided or even deliberately shoved aside. It is obvious that a great gulf still exists between the UN's actual capabilities and the strong organization which many desire it to be. That the United Nations is sought after in its capacities as agent and as forum in such a wide spectrum of political issues is primarily attributable to the fact that the organization can boast of almost perfect universality (with 191 states as members). Also important, however, is the UN's self-understanding as a broad global forum for international co-operation. This book is mainly about the administrative structure and functioninig of the United Nations Organisation.

1

Introduction

The United Nations (UN) is an international organization whose stated aims are to facilitate co-operation in international law, international security, economic development, social progress, human rights, and achieving world peace. The UN was founded in 1945 after World War II to replace the League of Nations, to stop wars between countries and to provide a platform for dialogue.

There are currently 192 member states, including nearly every recognized independent state in the world. From its headquarters on international territory in New York City, the UN and its specialized agencies decide on substantive and administrative issues in regular meetings held throughout the year. The organization is divided into administrative bodies, primarily:

- The General Assembly (the main deliberative assembly);
- The Security Council (decides certain resolutions for peace and security);
- The Economic and Social Council (assists in promoting

international economic and social cooperation and development);

- The Secretariat (provides studies, information, and facilities needed by the UN);
- The International Court of Justice (the primary judicial organ).

Additional bodies deal with the governance of all other UN System agencies, such as the World Health Organization (WHO) and United Nations Children's Fund (UNICEF). The UN's most visible public figure is the Secretary-General, currently Ban Ki-moon of South Korea, who attained the post in 2007. The organization is financed from assessed and voluntary contributions from its member states, and has six official languages: Arabic, Chinese (Mandarin), English, French, Russian, and Spanish.

History

The UN was founded as a successor to the League of Nations, which was widely considered to have been ineffective in its role as an international governing body, as it had been unable to prevent World War II. The term "United Nations" was first used by Winston Churchill and Franklin D. Roosevelt, in the 1942 Declaration by United Nations, which united the Allied countries of WWII under the Atlantic Charter, and soon became a term widely used to refer to them. Declarations signed at wartime Allied conferences in 1943 espoused the idea of the UN, and in 1944, representatives of the major Allied powers met to elaborate on the plans at the Dumbarton Oaks Conference. Those and later talks outlined the organization's proposed purposes, membership, organs, and ideals in regards to peace, security, and cooperation.

On 25 April 1945, the UN Conference on International Organization began in San Francisco, attended by 50 governments and a number of NGOs involved in drafting the Charter of the United Nations. The UN officially came into existence on 24 October 1945 upon ratification of the Charter by the five permanent members of the Security Council— France, the Republic of China, the Soviet Union, the United Kingdom and the United States — and by a majority of the other 46 signatories. The first meetings of the General Assembly, with 51 nations represented, and the Security Council, took place in London in January 1946.

Organization

The United Nations system is based on five principal organs (formerly six - the Trusteeship Council suspended operations in 1994); the General Assembly, the Security Council, the Economic and Social Council (ECOSOC), the Secretariat, and the International Court of Justice. Four of the five principal organs are located at the main United Nations headquarters located on international territory in New York City. The International Court of Justice is located in The Hague, while other major agencies are based in the UN offices at Geneva, Vienna and Nairobi. Other UN instutitions are located throughout the world.

The six official languages of the United Nations, used in intergovernmental meetings and documents, are Arabic, Chinese, English, French, Russian and Spanish, while the Secretariat uses two working languages, English and French. Five of the official languages were chosen when the UN was founded; Arabic was added later in 1973. The United Nations Editorial Manual states that the standard for English language documents is British usage and Oxford spelling (en-gb-oed), and the Chinese writing standard is Simplified Chinese. This replaced Traditional Chinese in 1971 when the Republic of China (Taiwan)'s UN membership was succeeded by the People's Republic of China.

General Assembly

The General Assembly is the main deliberative assembly of the United Nations. Composed of all United Nations member states, the assembly meets in regular yearly sessions under a president elected from among the member states. Over a two-week period at the start of each session, all members have the opportunity to address the assembly. Traditionally, the Secretary-General makes the first statement, followed by the president of the assembly. The first session was convened on 10 January 1946 in the Westminster Central Hall in London and included representatives of 51 nations.

When the General Assembly votes on important questions, a two-thirds majority of those present and voting is required. Examples of important questions include: recommendations on peace and security; election of members to organs; admission, suspension, and expulsion of members; and, budgetary matters. All other questions are decided by majority vote. Each member country has one vote. Apart from approval of budgetary matters, resolutions are not binding on the members. The Assembly may make recommendations on any matters within the scope of the UN, except matters of peace and security that are under Security Council consideration.

Conceivably, the one state, one vote power structure could enable states comprising just eight percent of the world population to pass a resolution by a two-thirds vote. However, as no more than recommendations, it is difficult to imagine a situation in which a recommendation by member states constituting just eight percent of the world's population, would be adhered to by the remaining ninety-two percent of the population, should they object.

Security Council

The Security Council is charged with maintaining peace and security among countries. While other organs of the United Nations can only make 'recommendations' to member governments, the Security Council has the power to make binding decisions that member governments have agreed to carry out, under the terms of Charter Article 25. The decisions of the Council are known as United Nations Security Council resolutions.

The Security Council is made up of 15 member states, consisting of five permanent seats and ten temporary seats. The permanent five are China, France, Russia, the United Kingdom and the United States. These members hold veto power over substantive but not procedural resolutions allowing a permanent member to block adoption but not to block the debate of a resolution unacceptable to it. The ten temporary seats are held for two-year terms with member states voted in by the General Assembly on a regional basis. The presidency of the Security Council is rotated alphabetically each month.

The Security Council has been criticised for being

unable to act in a clear and decisive way when confronted with a crisis.

Secretariat

The United Nations Secretariat is headed by the Secretary-General, assisted by a staff of international civil servants worldwide. It provides studies, information, and facilities needed by United Nations bodies for their meetings. It also carries out tasks as directed by the UN Security Council, the UN General Assembly, the UN Economic and Social Council, and other UN bodies. The United Nations Charter provides that the staff be chosen by application of the "highest standards of efficiency, competence, and integrity," with due regard for the importance of recruiting on a wide geographical basis.

The Charter provides that the staff shall not seek or receive instructions from any authority other than the UN. Each UN member country is enjoined to respect the international character of the Secretariat and not seek to influence its staff. The Secretary-General alone is responsible for staff selection.

The Secretary-General's duties include helping resolve international disputes, administering peacekeeping operations, organizing international conferences, gathering information on the implementation of Security Council decisions, and consulting with member governments regarding various initiatives. Key Secretariat offices in this area include the Office of the Coordinator of Humanitarian Affairs and the Department of Peacekeeping Operations. The Secretary-General may bring to the attention of the Security

Council any matter that, in his or her opinion, may threaten international peace and security.

Secretary-General

The Secretariat is headed by the Secretary-General, who acts as the *de facto* spokesman and leader of the UN. The current Secretary-General is Ban Ki-moon, who took over from Kofi Annan in 2007 and will be eligible for reappointment when his first term expires in 2011.

Envisioned by Franklin D. Roosevelt as a "world moderator", the position is defined in the UN Charter as the organization's "chief administrative officer", but the Charter also states that the Secretary-General can bring to the Security Council's attention "any matter which in his opinion may threaten the maintenance of international peace and security", giving the position greater scope for action on the world stage. The position has evolved into a dual role of an administrator of the UN organization, and a diplomat and mediator addressing disputes between member states and finding consensus to global issues.

The Secretary-General is appointed by the General Assembly, after being recommended by the Security Council. The selection can be vetoed by any member of the Security Council, and the General Assembly can theoretically override the Security Council's recommendation if a majority vote is not achieved, although this has not happened so far. There are no specific criteria for the post, but over the years it has become accepted that the post shall be held for one or two terms of five years, that the post shall be appointed based on geographical rotation, and that the Secretary-General shall not originate from one of the five permanent Security Council member states.

Secretaries-General of the United Nations					
No.	Name	Country of origin	Took office	Left office	Note
1	**Trygve Lie**	Norway	2 February 1946	10 November 1952	Resigned
2	**Dag Hammarskjöld**	Sweden	10 April 1953	18 September 1961	Died while in office
3	**U Thant**	Burma	30 November 1961	1 January 1972	First Secretary-General from Asia
4	**Kurt Waldheim**	Austria	1 January 1972	1 January 1982	
5	**Javier Pérez de Cuéllar**	Peru	1 January 1982	1 January 1992	First Secretary-General from South America
6	**Boutros Boutros-Ghali**	Egypt	1 January 1992	1 January 1997	First Secretary-General from Africa
7	**Kofi Annan**	Ghana	1 January 1997	1 January 2007	
8	**Ban Ki-moon**	South Korea	1 January 2007	Incumbent	

International Court of Justice

The International Court of Justice (ICJ), located in The Hague, Netherlands, is the primary judicial organ of the United Nations. Established in 1945 by the United Nations Charter, the Court began work in 1946 as the successor to the Permanent Court of International Justice. The Statute of the International Court of Justice, similar to that of its predecessor, is the main constitutional document constituting and regulating the Court.

It is based in the Peace Palace in The Hague, Netherlands, sharing the building with the Hague Academy of International Law, a private centre for the study of international law. Several of the Court's current judges are either alumni or former faculty members of the Academy. Its purpose is to adjudicate disputes among states. The court has heard cases related to war crimes, illegal state interference and ethnic cleansing, among others, and continues to hear cases. A related court, the International Criminal Court (ICC), began operating in 2002 through international discussions initiated by the General Assembly. It is the first permanent international court charged with trying those who commit the most serious crimes under international law, including war crimes and genocide. The ICC is functionally independent of the UN in terms of personnel and financing, but some meetings of the ICC governing body, the Assembly of States Parties to the Rome Statute, are held at the UN. There is a "relationship agreement" between the ICC and the UN that governs how the two institutions regard each other legally.

Economic and Social Council

The Economic and Social Council (ECOSOC) assists the General Assembly in promoting international economic and social cooperation and development. ECOSOC has 54 members, all of whom are elected by the General Assembly for a three-year term. The president is elected for a one-year term and chosen amongst the small or middle powers represented on ECOSOC. ECOSOC meets once a year in July for a four-week session. Since 1998, it has held another meeting each April with finance ministers heading key committees of the World Bank and the International Monetary Fund (IMF). Viewed separate from the specialized bodies it coordinates, ECOSOC's functions include information gathering, advising member nations, and making recommendations. In addition, ECOSOC is well-positioned to provide policy coherence and coordinate the overlapping functions of the UN's subsidiary bodies and it is in these roles that it is most active.

Specialized Institutions

There are many UN organizations and agencies that function to work on particular issues. Some of the most well-known agencies are the International Atomic Energy Agency, the Food and Agriculture Organization, UNESCO (United Nations Educational, Scientific and Cultural Organization), the World Bank and the World Health Organization.

The United Nations Charter stipulates that each primary organ of the UN can establish various specialized agencies to fulfill its duties.

Membership

An animation showing the timeline of accession of UN member states, *according to the UN*. Note that Antarctica has no government; political control of Western Sahara is in dispute; and the territories administered by the Republic of China (Taiwan) and Kosovo are considered by the UN to be provinces of the People's Republic of China and Republic of Serbia, respectively.

With the addition of Montenegro on 28 June 2006, there are currently 192 United Nations member states, including all fully recognized independent states apart from Vatican City, which has observer status.

The United Nations Charter outlines the rules for membership:

1. Membership in the United Nations is open to all other peace-loving states which accept the obligations contained in the present Charter and, in the judgment of the Organization, are able and willing to carry out these obligations.
2. The admission of any such state to membership in the United Nations will be effected by a decision of the General Assembly upon the recommendation of the Security Council.

The Group of 77 at the UN is a loose coalition of developing nations, designed to promote its members' collective economic interests and create an enhanced joint negotiating capacity in the United Nations. There were 77 founding members of the organization, but the organization has since expanded to 130 member countries. The group was founded on 15 June 1964 by the "Joint Declaration of the Seventy-Seven Countries" issued at the United Nations Conference on Trade and Development (UNCTAD). The first major meeting was in Algiers in 1967, where the *Charter of Algiers* was adopted and the basis for permanent institutional structures was begun.

Functions

Peacekeeping and Security

UN peacekeeping missions. Dark blue regions indicate

current missions, while light blue regions represent former missions.

The UN, after approval by the Security Council, sends peacekeepers to regions where armed conflict has recently ceased or paused to enforce the terms of peace agreements and to discourage combatants from resuming hostilities. Since the UN does not maintain its own military, peacekeeping forces are voluntarily provided by member states of the UN. The forces, also called the "Blue Helmets", who enforce UN accords are awarded United Nations Medals, which are considered international decorations instead of military decorations. The peacekeeping force as a whole received the Nobel Peace Prize in 1988.

The founders of the UN had envisaged that the organization would act to prevent conflicts between nations and make future wars impossible, however the outbreak of the Cold War made peacekeeping agreements extremely difficult due to the division of the world into hostile camps. Following the end of the Cold War, there were renewed calls for the UN to become the agency for achieving world peace, as there are several dozen ongoing conflicts that continue to rage around the globe.

A 2005 RAND Corp study found the UN to be successful in two out of three peacekeeping efforts. It compared UN nation-building efforts to those of the United States, and found that seven out of eight UN cases are at peace, as opposed to four out of eight US cases at peace. . Also in 2005, the Human Security Report documented a decline in the number of wars, genocides and human rights abuses since the end of the Cold War, and presented evidence, albeit circumstantial, that international activism — mostly spearheaded by the UN — has been the main cause of the decline in armed conflict since the end of the Cold War. Situations where the UN has not only acted to keep the peace but also occasionally intervened include the Korean War (1950-1953), and the authorization of intervention in Iraq after the Iraqi invasion of Kuwait in 1990. The UN has also drawn criticism for perceived failures. In many cases member states have shown reluctance to achieve or enforce Security Council resolutions, an issue that stems from the UN's intergovernmental nature — seen by some as simply an association of 192 member states who must reach consensus, not an independent organization. Disagreements in the Security Council about military action and intervention are seen as having failed to prevent the 1994 Rwandan Genocide, failed to provide humanitarian aid and intervene in the Second Congo War, failed to intervene in the 1995 Srebrenica massacre and protect a refugee haven by the authorising the peacekeepers to use force, failure to deliver food to starving people in Somalia, failure to implement provisions of Security Council resolutions related to the Israeli-Palestinian conflict, and continuing failure to prevent genocide or provide assistance in Darfur.

In addition to peacekeeping, the UN is also active in encouraging disarmament. Regulation of armaments was included in the writing of the UN Charter in 1945 and was envisioned as a way of limiting the use of human and economic resources for the creation of them. However, the advent of nuclear weapons came only weeks after the signing of the charter and immediately halted concepts of arms limitation and disarmament, resulting in the first resolution of the first ever General Assembly meeting calling for specific proposals for "the elimination from national armaments of atomic weapons and of all other major weapons adaptable to mass destruction". The principal forums for disarmament issues are the General Assembly First Committee, the UN Disarmament Commission, and the Conference on Disarmament, and considerations have been made of the merits of a ban on testing nuclear weapons, outer space arms control, the banning of chemical weapons and land mines, nuclear and conventional disarmament, nuclear-weapon-free zones, the reduction of military budgets, and measures to strengthen international security.

Human Rights and Humanitarian Assistance

The pursuit of human rights was a central reason for creating the UN. World War II atrocities and genocide led to a ready consensus that the new organization must work to prevent any similar tragedies in the future. An early objective was creating a legal framework for considering and acting on complaints about human rights violations. The UN Charter obliges all member nations to promote "universal respect for, and observance of, human rights" and to take "joint and separate action" to that end. The Universal Declaration of Human Rights, though not legally binding, was adopted by the General Assembly in 1948 as a common standard of achievement for all. The Assembly regularly takes up human rights issues.

The UN and its agencies are central in upholding and implementing the principles enshrined in the Universal Declaration of Human Rights. A case in point is support by the UN for countries in transition to democracy. Technical assistance in providing free and fair elections, improving judicial structures, drafting constitutions, training human rights officials, and transforming armed movements into political parties have contributed significantly to democratization worldwide. The UN has helped run elections in countries with little democratic history, including recently in Afghanistan and East Timor. The UN is also a forum to support the right of women to participate fully in the political, economic, and social life of their countries. The UN contributes to raising consciousness of the concept of human rights through its covenants and its attention to specific abuses through its General Assembly, Security Council resolutions, or International Court of Justice rulings.

The purpose of the United Nations Human Rights Council, established in 2006, is to address human rights violations. The Council is the successor to the United Nations Commission on Human Rights, which was often criticised for the high-profile positions it gave to member states that did not guarantee the human rights of their own citizens The council has 47 members distributed by region, which each serve three year terms, and may not serve three consecutive terms. A candidate to the body must be approved by a majority of the General Assembly. In addition, the council has strict rules for membership, including a universal human rights review. While some members with questionable human rights records have been elected, it is fewer than before with the increased focus on each member state's human rights record.

The rights of some 370 million indigenous peoples

around the world is also a focus for the UN, with a Declaration on the Rights of Indigenous Peoples being approved by the General Assembly in 2007. The declaration outlines the individual and collective rights to culture, language, education, identity, employment and health, thereby addressing post-colonial issues which had confronted indigenous peoples for centuries. The declaration aims to maintain, strengthen and encourage the growth of indigenous institutions, cultures and traditions. It also prohibits discrimination against indigenous peoples and promotes their active participation in matters which concern their past, present and future.

In conjunction with other organizations such as the Red Cross, the UN provides food, drinking water, shelter and other humanitarian services to populaces suffering from famine, displaced by war, or afflicted by other disasters. Major humanitarian branches of the UN are the World Food Programme (which helps feed more than 100 million people a year in 80 countries), the office of the High Commissioner for Refugees with projects in over 116 countries, as well as peacekeeping projects in over 24 countries.

Social and Economic Development

Millennium Development Goals:

1. eradicate extreme poverty and hunger;
2. achieve universal primary education;
3. promote gender equality and empower women;
4. reduce child mortality;
5. improve maternal health;
6. combat HIV/AIDS, malaria, and other diseases;
7. ensure environmental sustainability; and
8. develop a global partnership for development.

The UN is involved in supporting development, e.g. by the formulation of the Millennium Development Goals. The UN Development Programme (UNDP) is the largest multilateral source of grant technical assistance in the world. Organizations like the World Health Organization (WHO), UNAIDS, and The Global Fund to Fight AIDS, Tuberculosis and Malaria are leading institutions in the battle against diseases around the world, especially in poor countries. The UN Population Fund is a major provider of reproductive services. It has helped reduce infant and maternal mortality in 100 countries.

The UN also promotes human development through various related agencies. The World Bank Group and International Monetary Fund (IMF), for example, are independent, specialized agencies and observers within the UN framework, according to a 1947 agreement. They were initially formed as separate from the UN through the Bretton Woods Agreement in 1944.

The UN annually publishes the Human Development Index (HDI), a comparative measure ranking countries by poverty, literacy, education, life expectancy, and other factors.

The Millennium Development Goals are eight goals that all 192 United Nations member states have agreed to try to achieve by the year 2015. This was declared in the United Nations Millennium Declaration, signed in September 2000.

Other

Over the lifetime of the UN, over 80 colonies have attained independence. The General Assembly adopted the Declaration on the Granting of Independence to Colonial

Countries and Peoples in 1960 with no votes against but abstentions from all major colonial powers. Through the UN Committee on Decolonization, created in 1962, the UN has focused considerable attention on decolonization. It has also supported the new states that have arisen as a result self-determination initiatives. The committee has overseen the decolonization of every country larger than 20,000 km^2 and removed them from the United Nations list of Non-Self-Governing Territories, besides Western Sahara, a country larger than the UK only relinquished by Spain in 1975. The UN declares and coordinates international observances, periods of time to observe some issue of international interest or concern. Using the symbolism of the UN, a specially designed logo for the year, and the infrastructure of the United Nations System, various days and years have become catalysts to advancing key issues of concern on a global scale. For example, World Tuberculosis Day, Earth Day and International Year of Deserts and Desertification.

Funding

Main donators to the UN budget, 2006

Member state	Contribution(% of UN budget)
United States	22.00%
Japan	16.624%
Germany	8.66%
United Kingdom	6.13%
France	6.03%
Italy	4.89%
Canada	2.81%
China	2.667%
Spain	2.52%

Mexico	1.88%
Australia	1.59%
Brazil	1.52%
Other member states	22.679%

The UN is financed from assessed and voluntary contributions from member states. The regular two-year budgets of the UN and its specialized agencies are funded by assessments. The General Assembly approves the regular budget and determines the assessment for each member. This is broadly based on the relative capacity of each country to pay, as measured by their Gross National Income (GNI), with adjustments for external debt and low per capita income.

The Assembly has established the principle that the UN should not be overly dependent on any one member to finance its operations. Thus, there is a 'ceiling' rate, setting the maximum amount any member is assessed for the regular budget. In December 2000, the Assembly revised the scale of assessments to reflect current global circumstances. As part of that revision, the regular budget ceiling was reduced from 25% to 22%. The U.S. is the only member that has met the ceiling. In addition to a ceiling rate, the minimum amount assessed to any member nation (or 'floor' rate) is set at 0.001% of the UN budget. Also, for the least developed countries (LDC), a ceiling rate of 0.01% is applied.

The current operating budget is estimated at $4.19 billion (refer to table for major contributors).

A large share of UN expenditures addresses the core UN mission of peace and security. The peacekeeping budget for the 2005-2006 fiscal year is approximately $5 billion (compared to approximately $1.5 billion for the UN core budget over the same period), with some 70,000 troops deployed in 17 missions around the world. UN peace operations are funded by assessments, using a formula derived from the regular funding scale, but including a weighted surcharge for the five permanent Security Council members, who must approve all peacekeeping operations. This surcharge serves to offset discounted peacekeeping assessment rates for less developed countries. As of 1 January 2008, the top 10 providers of assessed financial contributions to United Nations peacekeeping operations were: the United States, Japan, Germany, the United Kingdom, France, Italy, China, Canada, Spain and the Republic of Korea.

Special UN programmes not included in the regular budget (such as UNICEF and UNDP) are financed by voluntary contributions from member governments. Most of this is financial contributions, but some is in the form of agricultural commodities donated for afflicted populations.

Personnel Policy

The UN and its agencies are immune to the laws of the countries where they operate, safeguarding UN's impartiality with regard to the host and member countries. This independence allows agencies to implement human resources policies that may even be contrary to the laws of a host - or a member country.

Despite their independence in matters of human resources policy, the UN and its agencies voluntarily apply the laws of member states regarding same-sex marriages, allowing decisions about the status of employees in a same-sex partnership to be based on nationality. The UN and its agencies recognize same-sex marriages only if the employees are citizens of countries that recognize the marriage. This practice is not specific to the recognition of same-sex marriage but reflects a common practice of the UN for a number of human resources matters. It has to be noted though that some agencies provide limited benefits to domestic partners of their staff and that some agencies do not recognise same-sex marriage or domestic partnership of their staff.

Reform

Proposed logo for a United Nations Parliamentary Assembly, which would involve direct election of a country's representative by its citizens

Since its founding, there have been many calls for reform of the United Nations, although little consensus on how to do so. Some want the UN to play a greater or more effective role in world affairs, while others want its role reduced to humanitarian work. There have also been numerous calls for the UN Security Council's membership to be increased, for different ways of electing the UN's Secretary-General, and for a United Nations Parliamentary Assembly.

The UN has also been accused of bureaucratic inefficiency and waste. During the 1990s the United States withheld dues citing inefficiency, and only started repayment on the condition that a major reforms initiative was introduced. In 1994, the Office of Internal Oversight Services (OIOS) was established by the General Assembly to serve as an efficiency watchdog.

An official reform programme was begun by Kofi

Annan in 1997. Reforms mentioned include changing the permanent membership of the Security Council (which currently reflects the power relations of 1945), making the bureaucracy more transparent, accountable and efficient, making the UN more democratic, and imposing an international tariff on arms manufacturers worldwide.

In September 2005, the UN convened a World Summit that brought together the heads of most member states, calling the summit "a once-in-a-generation opportunity to take bold decisions in the areas of development, security, human rights and reform of the United Nations." Kofi Annan had proposed that the summit agree on a global "grand bargain" to reform the UN, renewing the organization's focus on peace, security, human rights and development, and to make it better equipped at facing 21st century issues. The result of the summit was aa compromise text agreed on by world leaders, which included the creation of a Peacebuilding Commission to help countries emerging from conflict, a Human Rights Council, and a democracy fund, a clear and unambiguous condemnation of terrorism "in all its forms and manifestations", and agreements to devote more resources to the Office of Internal Oversight Services, to spend billions more on achieving the Millennium Development Goals, to wind up the Trusteeship Council due to the completion of its mission, and that the international community has a "responsibility to protect" - the duty to intervene in when national governments fail to fulfill their responsibility to protect their citizens from atrocious crimes.

The Office of Internal Oversight Services is being restructured to more clearly define its scope and mandate, and will receive more resources. In addition, to improve the oversight and auditing capabilities of the General Assembly, an Independent Audit Advisory Committee (IAAC) is being created. In June 2007, the Fifth Committee created a draft resolution for the terms of reference of this committee. An ethics office was established in 2006, responsible for administering new financial disclosure and whistleblower protection policies. Working with the OIOS, the ethics office also plans to implement a policy to avoid fraud and corruption. The Secretariat is in the process of reviewing all UN mandates that are more than five years old. The review is intended to determine which duplicative or unnecessary programmes should be eliminated. Not all member states are in agreement as to which of the over 7000 mandates should be reviewed. The dispute centres on whether mandates that have been renewed should be examined. As of September 2007, the process is ongoing.

Controversy and Criticism

There has been controversy and criticism of the UN organization and its activities since at least the 1950s. In the United States, an early opponent of the UN was the John Birch Society, which began a "get US out of the UN" campaign in 1959, charging that the UN's aim was to establish a "One World Government." In 1967, Richard Nixon, while running for President of the United States, criticized the UN as "obsolete and inadequate" for dealing with then-present crises like the Cold War. Jeane Kirkpatrick, who was appointed by Ronald Reagan to be United States Ambassador to the United Nations, wrote in a 1983 opinion piece in *The New York Times* that the process of discussions at the Security

Council "more closely resembles a mugging" of the United States "than either a political debate or an effort at problem solving." In a February 2003 speech, soon before the United States invasion of Iraq (for which he had been unable to get UN approval), George W. Bush said, "free nations will not allow the United Nations to fade into history as an ineffective, irrelevant debating society." In 2005, Bush appointed John R. Bolton to the position of Acting U.S. Ambassador to the UN; Bolton had made several statements critical of the UN, including saying, in 1994, "There is no such thing as the United Nations. There is only the international community, which can only be led by the only remaining superpower, which is the United States."

Accusations of Bias in the Arab-Israeli Conflict

Issues relating to the state of Israel, the Palestinian people and other aspects of the Arab-Israeli conflict occupy a large amount of debate time, resolutions and resources at the United Nations.

The adoption of UNSCOP's recommendation to partition Palestine by the United Nations General Assembly in 1947 was one of the earliest decisions of the UN. Since then, it maintained a central role in this region, especially by providing support for Palestinian refugees via the UNRWA and by providing a platform for Palestinian political claims via the CEIRPP, the UNDPR, the SCIIP, the UNISPAL and the International Day of Solidarity with the Palestinian People. The UN has sponsored several peace negotiations between the parties, the latest being the 2002 Road map for peace.

In recent years, the Middle East was the subject of

76% of country-specific UNGA resolutions, 100% of the Human Rights Council resolutions, 100% of the Commission on the Status of Women resolutions, 50% of reports from the World Food Program, 6% of Security Council resolutions and 6 of the 10 Emergency sessions. Of note is Resolution 3379 (1975) stating that "zionism is racism"; it was rescinded in 1991. These decisions, passed with the support of the OIC countries, invariably criticize Israel for her treatment of Palestinians. Many have qualified this degree of criticism as excessive. In particular, the UNHRC was widely criticized in 2007 for failing to condemn other human rights abusers besides Israel.

The United States has been criticized as well as supported for vetoing most UNSC decisions critical of Israel on the basis of their biased language, the so-called Negroponte doctrine.

Since 1961, Israel has been barred from the Asia regional group. In 2000, she was accepted within the WEOG group. The UNRWA has been accused of perpetuating the plight of Palestinian refugees. Although the UN condemns antisemitism, it has be accused of tolerating antisemitic remarks within its walls. Some argue that disproportional criticism of Israel constitutes a new form of antisemitism. UN personnel have been accused of participating directly in the armed conflict on several occasions.

Oil-for-Food Programme

The Oil-for-Food Programme was established by the UN in 1996 to allow Iraq to sell oil on the world market in exchange for food, medicine, and other humanitarian needs of ordinary Iraqi citizens who were affected by international economic sanctions, without allowing the Iraqi government to rebuild its military in the wake of the first Gulf War. Over $65 billion worth of Iraqi oil was sold on the world market. Officially, about $46 billion was used for humanitarian needs. Additional revenue paid for Gulf War reparations through a Compensation Fund, UN administrative and operational costs for the Programme (2.2%), and the weapons inspection programme (0.8%).

The programme was discontinued in late 2003 amidst allegations of widespread abuse and corruption. Benon Sevan, the former director, was suspended and then resigned from the UN, as an interim progress report of a UN-sponsored investigation concluded that Sevan had accepted bribes from the Iraqi regime, and recommended that his UN immunity be lifted to allow for a criminal investigation. Beyond Sevan, Kojo Annan was alleged to have illegally procured Oil-for-Food contracts on behalf of the Swiss company Cotecna. India's foreign minister, K. Natwar Singh, was removed from office because of his role in the scandal. And the Cole Inquiry investigated whether the Australian Wheat Board breached any laws with its contracts with Iraq.

Abuse of Human Rights

Albin Kurti, an activist from Kosovo, has accused United Nations, who govern Kosovo since 1999, of persecuting and arresting him for political reasons. His statements are supported by international human rights organizations such as Amnesty International and International Helsinki Federation. The UN-appointed judge according to an Amnesty report "approached the prosecutor after the hearing—in the absence of either Albin Kurti or his court-appointed lawyer—to clarify what the prosecution would like to recommend in relation to his detention."

Other Controversies

- UN peacekeepers have been accused of child rape, sexual abuse or soliciting prostitutes during various peacekeeping missions, starting in 2003, in Congo, Haiti, Liberia, Sudan, Burundi and Ivory Coast.

2

United Nations System

While the United Nations is an international organization, the United Nations System is the whole network of international organizations, treaties and conventions that were created by the United Nations.

The United Nations System is based on five active principal organs (formerly six, the UN Trusteeship Council suspended operations in 1994):

- UN General Assembly
- UN Security Council
- UN Economic and Social Council
- UN Secretariat
- International Court of Justice

In addition separate organizations, often subordinate to the principal organs, have been created to solve specialized tasks.

Organizations of the United Nations System

One of the remarkable features of the UN system is the duplication of responsibility.

For example, frustrated by their inability to control the ECOSOC the Assembly's third-world majority created the Conference on Trade and Development to address special issues that ECOSOC was not addressing. (Basu, Rumki, "The United Nations: Structure and Functions of an International Organisation," Sterling Publishing, New Delhi, 1993.)

Likewise, but just as an example, UNODOC (UN Office on Drugs and Crime) reports to the Secretariat, ECOSOC has a Functional Commission on crime and a separate one on Drugs, and the Assembly oversees the Interregional Crime and Justice Research Institute. UN's Organisation Chart

Organizations of the General Assembly

- Main committees
- Other sessional committees
- Standing committees and ad hoc bodies
- Other subsidiary org

Some of the Programmes and Funds include:

- UNCTAD - United Nations Conference on Trade and Development
    - o ITC - International Trade Centre (UNCTAD/WTO)
- UNDCP - United Nations Drug Control Programme
- UNDP - United Nations Development Programme
    - o UNCDF - United Nations Capital Development Fund
    - o UNIFEM - United Nations Development Fund for Women
    - o UNV - United Nations Volunteers
- UNEP - United Nations Environment Programme
- UNFPA - United Nations Fund for Population Activities
- UNHCR -Office of the United Nations High Commissioner for Refugees

- UN-HABITAT
- UNICEF - United Nations Children's Fund
- WFP - World Food Programme
- UNRWA
- UNEP

Research and Training Institutes

- INSTRAW - International Research and Training Institute for the Advancement of Women
- UNICRI - United Nations Interregional Crime and Justice Research Institute
- UNITAR - United Nations Institute for Training and Research
- UNRISD - United Nations Research Institute for Social Development
- UNIDIR - United Nations Institute for Disarmament Research (Reports only to the General Assembly)

Other Entities

- COPUOS - United Nations Committee on the Peaceful Uses of Outer Space
- JIU - Joint Inspection Unit (oversight body of the United Nations system)
- OHCHR - Office of the United Nations High Commissioner for Human Rights
- UNOPS - United Nations Office for Project Services
- UNU - United Nations University
- UNOOSA - United Nations Office for Outer Space Affairs
- UNSSC - United Nations System Staff College
- UNAIDS - Joint United Nations Programme on HIV/AIDS
- UNRRA - United Nations Relief and Rehabilitation Administration (ceased to exist in 1949)

- UPEACE - United Nations Mandated University for Peace

Organizations of the Security Council

- Human Rights Council
- Military Staff Committee
- Standing Committee and ad hoc bodies
- International Criminal Tribunal for the Former Yugoslavia
- International Criminal Tribunal for Rwanda
- 1540 Committee - Committee established pursuant to UN Security Council Resolution 1540 (2004)
- Counter-terrorism committee - Committee established pursuant to UN Security Council Resolution 1373 (2001)
- Peacekeeping Operations and Missions
    - o MONUC - United Nations Mission in the Democratic Republic of Congo
    - o UNAVEM III - United Nations Angola Verification Mission III
    - o UNDOF - United Nations Disengagement Observer Force
    - o UNFICYP - United Nations Peacekeeping Force in Cyprus
    - o UNIFIL - United Nations Interim Force in Lebanon
    - o UNMEE - United Nations Mission in Ethiopia and Eritrea
    - o UNMIK - United Nations Interim Administration Mission in Kosovo
    - o UNMIL - United Nations Mission in Liberia
    - o UNMIS - United Nations Mission In Sudan
    - o UNMOGIP - United Nations Military Observer Group in India and Pakistan

- UNMOVIC - United Nations Monitoring, Verification and Inspection Commission
- UNOMIG - United Nations Observer Mission in Georgia
- UNOMSIL - United Nations Mission of Observers in Sierra Leone
- UNSMIH - United Nations Support Mission in Haiti
- UNTSO - United Nations Truce Supervision Organization
- UNMIN - United Nations Mission in Nepal

• Former Peacekeeping Operations and Missions
- ONUMOZ - United Nations Operation in Mozambique
- UNAMIR - United Nations Assistance Mission for Rwanda
- UNAMSIL - United Nations Mission in Sierra Leone
- UNCRO - United Nations Confidence Restoration Operation in Croatia
- UNIKOM - United Nations Iraq-Kuwait Observation Mission
- UNMIBH - United Nations Mission in Bosnia and Herzegovina
- UNMOP - United Nations Mission of Observers in Prevlaka
- UNMOT - United Nations Mission of Observers in Tajikistan
- UNSCOM - United Nations Special Commission (Iraq)
- UNTAET-United Nations Transitional Administration in East Timor
- UNTAC - United Nations Transitional Authority in Cambodia

Organizations of the Economic and Social Council

Functional Commissions

• Commission for Social Development

- Commission on Narcotic Drugs
- Commission on Crime Prevention and Criminal Justice
- Commission on Science and Technology for Development
- Commission on Sustainable Development
- Commission on the Status of Women
- Commission on Population and Development
- Statistical Commission
- United Nations Forum on Forests

Regional Commissions

- United Nations Economic Commission for Europe (ECE)
- United Nations Economic Commission for Africa (ECA)
- United Nations Economic Commission for Latin America and the Caribbean (ECLAC)
- United Nations Economic and Social Commission for Asia and the Pacific (ESCAP)
- United Nations Economic and Social Commission for Western Asia (ESCWA)

Specialized Agencies

The specialized agencies are autonomous organizations working with the United Nations and each other through the coordinating machinery of the Economic and Social Council.

- ILO - International Labour Organization
- FAO - Food and Agriculture Organization
- UNESCO - United Nations Educational, Scientific and Cultural Organization
- WHO - World Health Organization
- World Bank Group
  - o IBRD - International Bank for Reconstruction and Development
  - o IDA - International Development Association
  - o IFC - International Finance Corporation

  - o MIGA - Multilateral Investment Guarantee Agency
  - o ICSID - International Centre for Settlement of Investment Disputes
- IMF - International Monetary Fund
- ICAO - International Civil Aviation Organization
- IMO - International Maritime Organization
- ITU - International Telecommunication Union
- UPU - Universal Postal Union
- WMO - World Meteorological Organization
- WIPO - World Intellectual Property Organization
- IFAD - International Fund for Agricultural Development
- UNIDO - United Nations Industrial Development Organization
- IRO - International Refugee Organization (ceased to exist in 1952)
- INCB - International Narcotics Control Board
- UNWTO - World Tourism Organization

Other Entities

- Permanent Forum on Indigenous Issues (PFII)
- Sessional and Standing Committees Expert, ad hoc and related bodies

Organizations of the Secretariat

The United Nations Secretariat is led by the Secretary-General of the United Nations, who is currently Ban Ki-moon of South Korea.

- OSG - Office of the Secretary-General
- OIOS - Office of Internal Oversight Services
- OLA - Office of Legal Affairs
- DPA - Department of Political Affairs
- DDA - Department for Disarmament Affairs
- DPKO - Department of Peacekeeping Operations

- OCHA - Office for the Coordination of Humanitarian Affairs
- DESA - Department of Economic and Social Affairs
- DGACM - Department of General Assembly and Conference Management
- DPI - Department of Public Information
- DM - Department of Management
- OIP - Office of the Iraq Programme
- UNSECOORD - Office of the United Nations Security Coordinator
- OHRLLS - Office of the High Representative for the Least Developed Countries, Landlocked Developing Countries and Small Island Developing States
- ODC - Office on Drugs and Crime
- UNOG - UN Office at Geneva
- UNOV - UN Office at Vienna
- UNON - UN Office at Nairobi

Organization of the International Court of Justice Related Organizations

- IAEA - International Atomic Energy Agency. Reports to the Security Council and the General Assembly
- World Trade Organization - (WTO)
- ICC - International Criminal Court
- ISA - International Seabed Authority
- ITLOS - International Tribunal for the Law of the Sea [10]
- Standby High-Readiness Brigade - The UN's standing military force.
- UNSOG - Special Operations Group.

CEB (Chief Executives Board) & Senior Management Group

The CEB (Chief Executives Board) brings together on

a regular basis the executive heads of the organisations of the UN System, under the chairmanship of the Secretary-General of the UN. There is also a Senior Management Group, which co-ordinates the work of the UN Secretariat and the UN Programmes and Funds, but does not include the UN Specialised Agencies.

Purposes and Principles

Article 1

The Purposes of the United Nations are:

1. To maintain international peace and security, and to that end: to take effective collective measures for the prevention and removal of threats to the peace, and for the suppression of acts of aggression or other breaches of the peace, and to bring about by peaceful means, and in conformity with the principles of justice and international law, adjustment or settlement of international disputes or situations which might lead to a breach of the peace;
2. To develop friendly relations among nations based on respect for the principle of equal rights and self-determination of peoples, and to take other appropriate measures to strengthen universal peace;
3. To achieve international co-operation in solving international problems of an economic, social, cultural, or humanitarian character, and in promoting and encouraging respect for human rights and for fundamental freedoms for all without distinction as to race, sex, language, or religion; and
4. To be a centre for harmonizing the actions of nations in the attainment of these common ends.

Article 2

The Organization and its Members, in pursuit of the Purposes stated in Article 1, shall act in accordance with the following Principles.

1. The Organization is based on the principle of the sovereign equality of all its Members.
2. All Members, in order to ensure to all of them the rights and benefits resulting from membership, shall fulfill in good faith the obligations assumed by them in accordance with the present Charter.
3. All Members shall settle their international disputes by peaceful means in such a manner that international peace and security, and justice, are not endangered.
4. All Members shall refrain in their international relations from the threat or use of force against the territorial integrity or political independence of any state, or in any other manner inconsistent with the Purposes of the United Nations.
5. All Members shall give the United Nations every assistance in any action it takes in accordance with the present Charter, and shall refrain from giving assistance to any state against which the United Nations is taking preventive or enforcement action.
6. The Organization shall ensure that states which are not Members of the United Nations act in accordance with these Principles so far as may be necessary for the maintenance of international peace and security.
7. Nothing contained in the present Charter shall authorize the United Nations to intervene in matters which are essentially within the domestic jurisdiction of any state or shall require the Members to submit such matters to settlement under the present Charter; but this principle shall not prejudice the application of enforcement measures under Chapter VII.

Membership

Article 3

The original Members of the United Nations shall be the states which, having participated in the United Nations

Conference on International Organization at San Francisco, or having previously signed the Declaration by United Nations of 1 January 1942, sign the present Charter and ratify it in accordance with Article 110.

Article 4

1. Membership in the United Nations is open to all other peace-loving states which accept the obligations contained in the present Charter and, in the judgment of the Organization, are able and willing to carry out these obligations.
2. The admission of any such state to membership in the United Nations will be effected by a decision of the General Assembly upon the recommendation of the Security Council.

Article 5

A Member of the United Nations against which preventive or enforcement action has been taken by the Security Council may be suspended from the exercise of the rights and privileges of membership by the General Assembly upon the recommendation of the Security Council. The exercise of these rights and privileges may be restored by the Security Council.

Article 6

A Member of the United Nations which has persistently violated the Principles contained in the present Charter may be expelled from the Organization by the General Assembly upon the recommendation of the Security Council.

Organs

Article 7

1. There are established as the principal organs of the

United Nations:
a General Assembly
a Security Council
an Economic and Social Council
a Trusteeship Council
an International Court of Justice
and a Secretariat.

2. Such subsidiary organs as may be found necessary may be established in accordance with the present Charter.

Article 8

The United Nations shall place no restrictions on the eligibility of men and women to participate in any capacity and under conditions of equality in its principal and subsidiary organs.

The General Assembly

Composition

Article 9

1. The General Assembly shall consist of all the Members of the United Nations.
2. Each Member shall have not more than five representatives in the General Assembly.

Functions and Powers

Article 10

The General Assembly may discuss any questions or any matters within the scope of the present Charter or relating to the powers and functions of any organs provided for in the present Charter, and, except as provided in Article 12, may make recommendations to the Members of the United Nations or to the Security Council or to both on any such questions or matters.

Article 11

1. The General Assembly may consider the general principles of co-operation in the maintenance of international peace and security, including the principles governing disarmament and the regulation of armaments, and may make recommendations with regard to such principles to the Members or to the Security Council or to both.
2. The General Assembly may discuss any questions relating to the maintenance of international peace and security brought before it by any Member of the United Nations, or by the Security Council, or by a state which is not a Member of the United Nations in accordance with Article 35, paragraph 2, and, except as provided in Article 12, may make recommendations with regard to any such questions to the state or states concerned or to the Security Council or to both. Any such question on which action is necessary shall be referred to the Security Council by the General Assembly either before or after discussion.
3. The General Assembly may call the attention of the Security Council to situations which are likely to endanger international peace and security.
4. The powers of the General Assembly set forth in this Article shall not limit the general scope of Article 10.

Article 12

1. While the Security Council is exercising in respect of any dispute or situation the functions assigned to it in the present Charter, the General Assembly shall not make any recommendation with regard to that dispute or situation unless the Security Council so requests.
2. The Secretary-General, with the consent of the Security Council, shall notify the General Assembly at each session

of any matters relative to the maintenance of international peace and security which are being dealt with by the Security Council and shall similarly notify the General Assembly, or the Members of the United Nations if the General Assembly is not in session, immediately the Security Council ceases to deal with suchmatters.

Article 13

1. The General Assembly shall initiate studies and make recommendations for the purpose of:
   a. promoting international co-operation in the political field and encouraging the progressive development of international law and its codification;
   b. promoting international co-operation in the economic, social, cultural, educational, and health fields, and assisting in the realization of human rights and fundamental freedoms for all without distinction as to race, sex, language, or religion.
2. The further responsibilities, functions and powers of the General Assembly with respect to matters mentioned in paragraph 1 (b) above are set forth in Chapters IX and X.

Article 14

Subject to the provisions of Article 12, the General Assembly may recommend measures for the peaceful adjustment of any situation, regardless of origin, which it deems likely to impair the general welfare or friendly relations among nations, including situations resulting from a violation of the provisions of the present Charter setting forth the Purposes and Principles of the United Nations.

Article 15

1. The General Assembly shall receive and consider annual

and special reports from the Security Council; these reports shall include an account of the measures that the Security Council has decided upon or taken to maintain international peace and security.

2. The General Assembly shall receive and consider reports from the other organs of the United Nations.

Article 16

The General Assembly shall perform such functions with respect to the international trusteeship system as are assigned to it under Chapters XII and XIII, including the approval of the trusteeship agreements for areas not designated as strategic.

Article 17

1. The General Assembly shall consider and approve the budget of the Organization.
2. The expenses of the Organization shall be borne by the Members as apportioned by the General Assembly.
3. The General Assembly shall consider and approve any financial and budgetary arrangements with specialized agencies referred to in Article 57 and shall examine the administrative budgets of such specialized agencies with a view to making recommendations to the agencies concerned.

Voting

Article 18

1. Each member of the General Assembly shall have one vote.
2. Decisions of the General Assembly on important questions shall be made by a two-thirds majority of the members present and voting. These questions shall include: recommendations with respect to the maintenance of

international peace and security, the election of the non-permanent members of the Security Council, the election of the members of the Economic and Social Council, the election of members of the Trusteeship Council in accordance with paragraph 1 (c) of Article 86, the admission of new Members to the United Nations, the suspension of the rights and privileges of membership, the expulsion of Members, questions relating to the operation of the trusteeship system, and budgetary questions.

3. Decisions on other questions, including the determination of additional categories of questions to be decided by a two-thirds majority, shall be made by a majority of the members present and voting.

Article 19

A Member of the United Nations which is in arrears in the payment of its financial contributions to the Organization shall have no vote in the General Assembly if the amount of its arrears equals or exceeds the amount of the contributions due from it for the preceding two full years. The General Assembly may, nevertheless, permit such a Member to vote if it is satisfied that the failure to pay is due to conditions beyond the control of the Member.

Procedure

Article 20

The General Assembly shall meet in regular annual sessions and in such special sessions as occasion may require. Special sessions shall be convoked by the Secretary-General at the request of the Security Council or of a majority of the Members of the United Nations.

Article 21

The General Assembly shall adopt its own rules of procedure. It shall elect its President for each session.

Article 22

The General Assembly may establish such subsidiary organs as it deems necessary for the performance of its functions.

The Security Council

Composition

Article 23

1. The Security Council shall consist of fifteen Members of the United Nations. The Republic of China, France, the Union of Soviet Socialist Republics, the United Kingdom of Great Britain and Northern Ireland, and the United States of America shall be permanent members of the Security Council. The General Assembly shall elect ten other Members of the United Nations to be non-permanent members of the Security Council, due regard being specially paid, in the first instance to the contribution of Members of the United Nations to the maintenance of international peace and security and to the other purposes of the Organization, and also to equitable geographical distribution.
2. The non-permanent members of the Security Council shall be elected for a term of two years. In the first election of the non-permanent members after the increase of the membership of the Security Council from eleven to fifteen, two of the four additional members shall be chosen for a term of one year. A retiring member shall not be eligible for immediate re-election.

3. Each member of the Security Council shall have one representative.

Functions and Powers

Article 24

1. In order to ensure prompt and effective action by the United Nations,its Members confer on the Security Council primary responsibility for the maintenance of international peace and security, and agree that in carrying out its duties under this responsibility the Security Council acts on their behalf.
2. In discharging these duties the Security Council shall act in accordance with the Purposes and Principles of the United Nations. The specific powers granted to the Security Council for the discharge of these duties are laid down in Chapters VI, VII, VIII, and XII.
3. The Security Council shall submit annual and, when necessary, special reports to the General Assembly for its consideration.

Article 25

The Members of the United Nations agree to accept and carry out the decisions of the Security Council in accordance with the present Charter.

Article 26

In order to promote the establishment and maintenance of international peace and security with the least diversion for armaments of the world's human and economic resources, the Security Council shall be responsible for formulating, with the assistance of the Military Staff Committee referred to in Article 47, plans to be submitted to the Members of the United Nations for the establishment of a system for the regulation of armaments.

Voting

Article 27

1. Each member of the Security Council shall have one vote.
2. Decisions of the Security Council on procedural matters shall be made by an affirmative vote of nine members.
3. Decisions of the Security Council on all other matters shall be made by an affirmative vote of nine members including the concurring votes of the permanent members; provided that, in decisions under Chapter VI, and under paragraph 3 of Article 52, a party to a dispute shall abstain from voting.

Procedure

Article 28

1. The Security Council shall be so organized as to be able to function continuously. Each member of the Security Council shall for this purpose be represented at all times at the seat of the Organization.
2. The Security Council shall hold periodic meetings at which each of its members may, if it so desires, be represented by a member of the government or by some other specially designated representative.
3. The Security Council may hold meetings at such places other than the seat of the Organization as in its judgment will best facilitate its work.

Article 29

The Security Council may establish such subsidiary organs as it deems necessary for the performance of its functions.

Article 30

The Security Council shall adopt its own rules of procedure, including the method of selecting its President.

Article 31

Any Member of the United Nations which is not a member of the Security Council may participate, without vote, in the discussion of any question brought before the Security Council whenever the latter considers that the interests of that Member are specially affected.

Article 32

Any Member of the United Nations which is not a member of the Security Council or any state which is not a Member of the United Nations, if it is a party to a dispute under consideration by the Security Council, shall be invited to participate, without vote, in the discussion relating to the dispute. The Security Council shall lay down such conditions as it deems just for the participation of a state which is not a Member of the United Nations.

Pacific Settlement of Disputes

Article 33

1. The parties to any dispute, the continuance of which is likely to endanger the maintenance of international peace and security, shall, first of all, seek a solution by negotiation, enquiry, mediation, conciliation, arbitration, judicial settlement, resort to regional agencies or arrangements, or other peaceful means of their own choice.
2. The Security Council shall, when it deems necessary, call upon the parties to settle their dispute by such means.

Article 34

The Security Council may investigate any dispute, or any situation which might lead to international friction or give rise to a dispute, in order to determine whether the continuance of the dispute or situation is likely to endanger the maintenance of international peace and security.

Article 35

1. Any Member of the United Nations may bring any dispute, or any situation of the nature referred to in Article 34, to the attention of the Security Council or of the General Assembly.
2. A state which is not a Member of the United Nations may bring to the attention of the Security Council or of the General Assembly any dispute to which it is a party if it accepts in advance, for the purposes of the dispute, the obligations of pacific settlement provided in the present Charter.
3. The proceedings of the General Assembly in respect of matters brought to its attention under this Article will be subject to the provisions of Articles 11 and 12.

Article 36

1. The Security Council may, at any stage of a dispute of the nature referred to in Article 33 or of a situation of like nature, recommend appropriate procedures or methods of adjustment.
2. The Security Council should take into consideration any procedures for the settlement of the dispute which have already been adopted by the parties.
3. In making recommendations under this Article the Security Council should also take into consideration that legal disputes should as a general rule be referred by the parties to the International Court of Justice in

accordance with the provisions of the Statute of the Court.

Article 37

1. Should the parties to a dispute of the nature referred to in Article 33 fail to settle it by the means indicated in that Article, they shall refer it to the Security Council.
2. If the Security Council deems that the continuance of the dispute is in fact likely to endanger the maintenance of international peace and security, it shall decide whether to take action under Article 36 or to recommend such terms of settlement as it may consider appropriate.

Article 38

Without prejudice to the provisions of Articles 33 to 37, the Security Council may, if all the parties to any dispute so request, make recommendations to the parties with a view to a pacific settlement of the dispute.

Action with Respect to thereats to the Peace, Breaches of The Peace, and Acts of Aggression

Article 39

The Security Council shall determine the existence of any threat to the peace, breach of the peace, or act of aggression and shall make recommendations, or decide what measures shall be taken in accordance with Articles 41 and 42, to maintain or restore international peace and security.

Article 40

In order to prevent an aggravation of the situation, the Security Council may, before making the recommendations or deciding upon the measures provided for in Article 39, call upon the parties concerned to comply with such provisional measures as it deems necessary or desirable. Such provisional measures shall be without prejudice to the rights, claims, or position of the parties concerned. The Security Council shall duly take account of failure to comply with such provisional measures.

Article 41

The Security Council may decide what measures not involving the use of armed force are to be employed to give effect to its decisions, and it may call upon the Members of the United Nations to apply such measures.

These may include complete or partial interruption of economic relations and of rail, sea, air, postal, telegraphic, radio, and other means of communication, and the severance of diplomatic relations.

Article 42

Should the Security Council consider that measures provided for in Article 41 would be inadequate or have proved to be inadequate, it may take such action by air, sea, or land forces as may be necessary to maintain or restore international peace and security. Such action may include demonstrations, blockade, and other operations by air, sea, or land forces of Members of the United Nations.

Article 43

1. All Members of the United Nations, in order to contribute to the maintenance of international peace and security, undertake to make available to the Security Council, on its call and in accordance with a special agreement or agreements, armed forces, assistance, and facilities, including rights of passage, necessary for the purpose

of maintaining international peace and security.

2. Such agreement or agreements shall govern the numbers and types of forces, their degree of readiness and general location, and the nature of the facilities and assistance to be provided.

3. The agreement or agreements shall be negotiated as soon as possible on the initiative of the Security Council. They shall be concluded between the Security Council and Members or between the Security Council and groups of Members and shall be subject to ratification by the signatory states in accordance with their respective constitutional processes.

Article 44

When the Security Council has decided to use force it shall, before calling upon a Member not represented on it to provide armed forces in fulfilment of the obligations assumed under Article 43, invite that Member, if the Member so desires, to participate in the decisions of the Security Council concerning the employment of contingents of that Member's armed forces.

Article 45

In order to enable the United Nations to take urgent military measures, Members shall hold immediately available national air-force contingents for combined international enforcement action. The strength and degree of readiness of these contingents and plans for their combined action shall be determined within the limits laid down in the special agreement or agreements referred to in Article 43, by the Security Council with the assistance of the Military Staff Committee.

Article 46

Plans for the application of armed force shall be made by the Security Council with the assistance of the Military Staff Committee.

Article 47

1. There shall be established a Military Staff Committee to advise and assist the Security Council on all questions relating to the Security Council's military requirements for the maintenance of international peace and security, the employment and command of forces placed at its disposal, the regulation of armaments, and possible disarmament.
2. The Military Staff Committee shall consist of the Chiefs of Staff of the permanent members of the Security Council or their representatives. Any Member of the United Nations not permanently represented on the Committee shall be invited by the Committee to be associated with it when the efficient discharge of the Committee's responsibilities requires the participation of that Member in its work.
3. The Military Staff Committee shall be responsible under the Security Council for the strategic direction of any armed forces placed at the disposal of the Security Council. Questions relating to the command of such forces shall be worked out subsequently.
4. The Military Staff Committee, with the authorization of the Security Council and after consultation with appropriate regional agencies, may establish regional sub-committees.

Article 48

1. The action required to carry out the decisions of the

Security Council for the maintenance of international peace and security shall be taken by all the Members of the United Nations or by some of them, as the Security Council may determine.

2. Such decisions shall be carried out by the Members of the United Nations directly and through their action in the appropriate international agencies of which they are members.

Article 49

The Members of the United Nations shall join in affording mutual assistance in carrying out the measures decided upon by the Security Council.

Article 50

If preventive or enforcement measures against any state are taken by the Security Council, any other state, whether a Member of the United Nations or not, which finds itself confronted with special economic problems arising from the carrying out of those measures shall have the right to consult the Security Council with regard to a solution of those problems.

Article 51

Nothing in the present Charter shall impair the inherent right of individual or collective self-defence if an armed attack occurs against a Member of the United Nations, until the Security Council has taken measures necessary to maintain international peace and security. Measures taken by Members in the exercise of this right of self-defence shall be immediately reported to the Security Council and shall not in any way affect the authority and responsibility of the Security Council under the present Charter to take at any time such action as it deems necessary in order to maintain or restore international peace and security.

Regional Arrangements

Article 52

1. Nothing in the present Charter precludes the existence of regional arrangements or agencies for dealing with such matters relating to the maintenance of international peace and security as are appropriate for regional action provided that such arrangements or agencies and their activities are consistent with the Purposes and Principles of the United Nations.
2. The Members of the United Nations entering into such arrangements or constituting such agencies shall make every effort to achieve pacific settlement of local disputes through such regional arrangements or by such regional agencies before referring them to the Security Council.
3. The Security Council shall encourage the development of pacific settlement of local disputes through such regional arrangements or by such regional agencies either on the initiative of the states concerned or by reference from the Security Council.
4. This Article in no way impairs the application of Articles 34 and 35.

Article 53

1. The Security Council shall, where appropriate, utilize such regional arrangements or agencies for enforcement action under its authority. But no enforcement action shall be taken under regional arrangements or by regional agencies without the authorization of the Security Council, with the exception of measures against any enemy state, as defined in paragraph 2 of this Article,

provided for pursuant to Article 107 or in regional arrangements directed against renewal of aggressive policy on the part of any such state, until such time as the Organization may, on request of the Governments concerned, be charged with the responsibility for preventing further aggression by such a state.

2. The term enemy state as used in paragraph 1 of this Article applies to any state which during the Second World War has been an enemy of any signatory of the present Charter.

Article 54

The Security Council shall at all times be kept fully informed of activities undertaken or in contemplation under regional arrangements or by regional agencies for the maintenance of international peace and security.

International Economic and Social Co-operation

Article 55

With a view to the creation of conditions of stability and well-being which are necessary for peaceful and friendly relations among nations based on respect for the principle of equal rights and self-determination of peoples, the United Nations shall promote:

a. higher standards of living, full employment, and conditions of economic and social progress and development;

b. solutions of international economic, social, health, and related problems; and international cultural and educational cooperation; and

c. universal respect for, and observance of, human rights and fundamental freedoms for all without distinction as to race, sex, language, or religion.

Article 56

All Members pledge themselves to take joint and separate action in co-operation with the Organization for the achievement of the purposes set forth in Article 55.

Article 57

1. The various specialized agencies, established by intergovernmental agreement and having wide international responsibilities, as defined in their basic instruments, in economic, social, cultural, educational, health, and related fields, shall be brought into relationship with the United Nations in accordance with the provisions of Article 63.
2. Such agencies thus brought into relationship with the United Nations are hereinafter referred to as specialized agencies.</OL.

Article 58

The Organization shall make recommendations for the co-ordination of the policies and activities of the specialized agencies.

Article 59

The Organization shall, where appropriate, initiate negotiations among the states concerned for the creation of any new specialized agencies required for the accomplishment of the purposes set forth in Article 55.

Article 60

Responsibility for the discharge of the functions of the Organization set forth in this Chapter shall be vested in the General Assembly and, under the authority of the General Assembly, in the Economic and Social Council, which shall have for this purpose the powers set forth in Chapter X.

3

Functions and Powers of the General Assembly

Forum for Multilateral Negotiation

Established in 1945 under the Charter of the United Nations, the General Assembly occupies a central position as the chief deliberative, policy-making and representative organ of the United Nations. Comprising all 192 Members of the United Nations, it provides a forum for multilateral discussion of the full spectrum of international issues covered by the Charter. It also plays a significant role in the process of standard-setting and the codification of international law. The Assembly meets in regular session intensively from September to December each year, and thereafter as required.

Functions and Powers of the General Assembly

According to the Charter of the United Nations, the General Assembly may:

- Consider and make recommendations on the general principles of cooperation for maintaining international peace and security, including disarmament;

- Discuss any question relating to international peace and security and, except where a dispute or situation is currently being discussed by the Security Council, make recommendations on it;
- Discuss, with the same exception, and make recommendations on any questions within the scope of the Charter or affecting the powers and functions of any organ of the United Nations;
- Initiate studies and make recommendations to promote international political cooperation, the development and codification of international law, the realization of human rights and fundamental freedoms and international collaboration in the economic, social, humanitarian, cultural, educational and health fields;
- Make recommendations for the peaceful settlement of any situation that might impair friendly relations among nations;
- Receive and consider reports from the Security Council and other United Nations organs;
- Consider and approve the United Nations budget and establish the financial assessments of Member States;
- Elect the non-permanent members of the Security Council and the members of other United Nations councils and organs and, on the recommendation of the Security Council, appoint the Secretary-General.

Pursuant to its "Uniting for Peace" resolution of November 1950 (resolution 377 (V)), the Assembly may also take action if the Security Council fails to act, owing to the negative vote of a permanent member, in a case where there appears to be a threat to the peace, breach of the peace or act of aggression. The Assembly can consider the matter immediately with a view to making recommendations to Members for collective measures to maintain or restore international peace and security (see "Special sessions and emergency special sessions" below).

While the Assembly is empowered to make only non-binding recommendations to States on international issues within its competence, it has, nonetheless, initiated actions — political, economic, humanitarian, social and legal—which have affected the lives of millions of people throughout the world. The landmark Millennium Declaration, adopted in 2000, and the 2005 World Summit Outcome Document, reflect the commitment of Member States to reach specific goals to attain peace, security and disarmament along with development and poverty eradication; safeguard human rights and promote the rule of law; protect our common environment; meet the special needs of Africa; and strengthen the United Nations.

The Search for Consensus

Each Member State in the Assembly has one vote. Votes taken on designated important issues, such as recommendations on peace and security and the election of Security Council members, require a two-thirds majority of Member States, but other questions are decided by simple majority.

In recent years, a special effort has been made to achieve consensus on issues, rather than deciding by a formal vote, thus strengthening support for the Assembly's decisions. The President, after having consulted and reached agreement with delegations, can propose that a resolution be adopted without a vote.

Subsidiary Organs of the General Assembly

Boards

- Board of Auditors [established by GA Resolution 74 (I)]
- Trade and Development Board [established by GA Resolution 1995 (XIX)]
- United Nations Joint Staff Pension Board [established by GA Resolution 248 (III)]

Executive Boards

- Executive Board of the United Nations Children's Fund [established by GA Resolution 57 (I) and 48/162]
- Executive Board of the United Nations Development Programme and of the United Nations Population Fund [established by GA Resolution 2029 (XX) and 48/162]
- Executive Board of the World Food Programme [established by GA Resolution 50/8]

Commissions

- Disarmament Commission [established by GA Resolution 502 (VI) and S-10/2]
- International Civil Service Commission [established by GA Resolution 3357 (XXIX)]
- International Law Commission [established by GA Resolution 174 (II)]
- United Nations Commission on International Trade Law (UNCITRAL) [established by GA Resolution 2205 (XXI)]
- United Nations Conciliation Commission for Palestine [established by GA Resolution 194 (III)]
- United Nations Peacebuilding Commission [established by GA Resolution 60/180 and UN Securiy Council Resolutions 1645(2005) and 1646(2005)]

Advisory Commission

- Advisory Commission on the United Nations Relief And

Works Agency for Palestine Refugees in the Near East [established by GA Resolution 302 (IV)]

Committees

- Committee for the United Nations Population Award [established by GA Resolution 36/201]
- Committee on Contributions [established by GA Resolution 14 (I) A]
- Committee against Torture [established by GA Resolution 39/46 A]
- Committee for Programme and Coordination [established by GA Resolution 31/93 and ECOSOC Resolution 2008 (LX)]
- Committee on Conferences [established by GA Resolution 43/222B]
- Committee on Information [established by GA Resolution 33/115 C]
- Committee on Relations with the Host Country [established by GA Resolution 2819 (XXVI)]
- Committee on the Elimination of Discrimination against Women [established by GA Resolution 34/180 and 51/68]
- Committee on the Elimination of Racial Discrimination [established by GA Resolution 2106 A (XX)]
- Committee on the Exercise of the Inalienable Rights of the Palestinian People [established by GA Resolution 3376 (XXX)]
- Committee on the Peaceful Uses of Outer Space (COPUOS) [established by GA Resolution 1472 A (XIV)]
- Committee on the Rights of the Child [established by GA Resolution 44/25, 47/112 and 49/211]
- Consultative Committee on the United Nations Development Fund for Women [established by GA Resolution 31/133 and 39/125]

- Human Rights Committee [established by GA Resolution 2200 A (XXI)]
- United Nations Scientific Committee on the Effects of Atomic Radiation (UNSCEAR) [established by GA Resolution 913 (X)]

Ad hoc Committees

- Ad Hoc Committee Established by General Assembly Resolution 51/210 [established by GA Resolution 51/210]
- Ad Hoc Committee of the General Assembly for the Announcement of Voluntary Contributions to the Programme of the United Nations High Commissioner for Refugees [established by GA Resolution 1729 (XVI)]
- Ad Hoc Committee of the General Assembly for the Announcement of Voluntary Contributions to the United Nations Relief and Works Agency for Palestine Refugees in the Near East [established by GA Resolution 1729 (XVI)]
- Ad Hoc Committee on a Comprehensive and Integral International Convention on Protection and Promotion of the Rights and Dignity of Persons with Disabilities [established by GA Resolution 56/168]
- Ad Hoc Committee on the Elaboration of a Convention Against Corruption [established by GA Resolution 55/61]
- Ad Hoc Committee on the Indian Ocean [established by GA Resolution 2992 (XXVII)]
- Ad Hoc Committee on the Scope of Legal Protection under the Convention on the Safety of United Nations and Associated Personnel [established by GA Resolution 56/89]

Advisory Committees

- Advisory Committee on Administrative and Budgetary Questions [established by GA Resolution 173 (II)]

- Advisory Committee on the United Nations Programme of Assistance in the Teaching, Study, Dissemination and Wider Appreciation of International Law [established by GA Resolution 2099 (XX)]

Executive Committee

- Executive Committee of the Programme of the United Nations High Commissioner for Refugees [established by GA Resolution 1166 (XII)]

High-level Committee

- High-level Committee on the Review of Technical Cooperation among Developing Countries [established by GA Resolution 33/134]

Special Committees

- Special Committee on Peace-keeping Operations [established by GA Resolution 2006 (XIX)]
- Special Committee on the Charter of the United Nations and on the Strengthening of the Role of the Organization [established by GA Resolution 3349 (XXIX)]
- Special Committee on the Situation with regard to the Implementation of the Declaration on the Granting of Independence to Colonial Countries and Peoples [established by GA Resolution 1654 (XVI)]
- Special Committee to Investigate Israeli Practices Affecting the Human Rights of the Palestinian People and Other Arabs of the Occupied Territories [established by GA Resolution 2443 (XXIII)]

Councils

- Human Rights Council [established by GA Resolution 60/251]
- Council of the United Nations University [established by GA Resolution 3081 (XXVIII)]

Governing Councils

- Governing Council of the United Nations Environment Programme [established by GA Resolution 2997 (XXVII)]
- Governing Council of the United Nations Human Settlements Programme, UN - Habitat

  [In General Assembly resolution 56/206, the GA decided to transform the Commission on Human Settlements to the Governing Council of the UN Human Settlements Programme, UN-Habitat. GA Resolution 32/162 states the objectives, functions and responsibilities of the Governing Council.]

Panel

- Panel of External Auditors of the United Nations, the Specialized Agencies and the International Atomic Energy Agency [established by GA Resolution 347 (IV) and 1438 (XIV)]

Working Groups

- High-level Open-ended Working Group on the Financial Situation of the United Nations [established by GA Resolution 49/143]
- Working Group on the Future Operations of the International Research and Training Institute for the Advancement of Women [established by GA Resolution 56/125]
- Working Group on the Finance of the United Nations Relief and Works Agency for Palestine Refugees in the Near East (UNRWA) [established by GA Resolution 2656 (XXV)]

Open-ended Ad hoc Working Groups

- Open-ended Ad Hoc Working Group of the General Assembly on the Integrated and Coordinated Implementation of and Follow-up to the Major United Nations Conferences and Summits in the Economic and Social Fields [established by GA Resolution 57/270]

Open-ended Working Groups

- Open-ended Working Group on the Causes of Conflict and the Promotion of Durable Peace and Sustainable Development in Africa [established by GA Resolution 54/234]
- Open-ended Working Group on the Question of Equitable Representation on and Increase in the Membership of the Security Council and Other Matters Related to the Security Council [established by GA Resolution 48/26]
- Open-ended Working Group to consider the objectives and agenda, including the possible establishment of the preparatory committee, for the fourth special session of the General Assembly devoted to disarmament [established by GA Resolution 57/61]

Other

- Joint Inspection Unit [established by GA Resolution 2150 (XXI)]
- United Nations Administrative Tribunal [established by GA Resolution 351 (IV)]
- United Nations Open-ended Informal Consultative Process on Oceans and the Law of the Sea [established by GA Resolution 54/33 and 57/141]

Rules of Procedure

The Rules of procedure of the General Assembly - including amendments and additions adopted up to September 2007 - are now available in HTML.

The menu allows navigation through its 163 rules and its annexes.

1. At its first regular session, the General Assembly adopted provisional rules of procedure (A/71/Rev.1) based on a text contained in the report of the Preparatory Commission of the United Nations [PC/20, chap. I, sect. 3].
2. At the same session, the General Assembly, by resolution 102 (I) of 15 December 1946, established the Committee on Procedures and Organization, consisting of 15 Member States.
3. At its second session, the General Assembly considered the report of the Committee on Procedures and Organization [Official Records of the General Assembly, Second Session, Plenary Meetings, vol. II, annex IV, document A/388], which contained draft rules of procedure proposed by the Committee [See Official Records of the General Assembly, Set and Session, Plenary Meetings, document A/388, part III], and, by resolution 173 (II) of 17 November 1947, adopted its rules of procedure. These rules entered into force on 1 January 1948.
4. At the same session, the General Assembly, by resolution 116 (II) of 21 November 1947, decided to add new rules 113, 114, 116 and 117 [See Rules 134, 135, 137 and 138 of the present rules of procedure], relating to the admission of new Members.
5. At its third session, the General Assembly, by resolution 262 (III) of 11 December 1948, decided to include Spanish among its working languages and to amend accordingly rules 44 to 48 [See Rules 51 to 55 of the present rules of procedure].
6. At the same session, the General Assembly, by resolution 271 (III) of 29 April 1949, established the Special

Committee on Methods and Procedures of the General Assembly, consisting of 15 Member States.

7. At its fourth session, the General Assembly considered the recommendations contained in the report of the Special Committee on Methods and Procedures of the General Assembly [See Official Records of the General Assembly, Fourth Session, Supplement No. 12 (A/937)] and, by resolution 362 (IV) of 22 October 1949, decided:

   (a) To amend rules 14, 31, 33, 35, 59, 64, 65, 67, 68, 69, 72, 80, 81, 82, 97, 98, 102, 103, 105, 106, 107, 110, 117, 118 and 119 [Rules 15, 35, 38, 40, 66, 71, 72, 74, 75, 76, 79, 88, 89, 90, 106, 108, 113, 114, 116, 117, 118, 121, 128, 129 and 130 of the present rules of procedure].

   (b) To add new rules 1A, 19, 19B, 19C, 31A, 35A, 35B, 56A, 89A and 97A [Rules 2, 20, 22, 23, 36, 41, 42, 62, 99 and 107 of the present rules of procedure].

   By the same resolution, the General Assembly adopted several of the recommendations and suggestions of the Special Committee and requested the Secretary-General to prepare a document embodying these recommendations and suggestions in a convenient form for use by the General Committee and delegations of Member States in the Assembly. The text of these recommendations and suggestions is reproduced in annex I.

8. At the same session, the General Assembly, by resolution 366 (IV) of 3 December 1949, adopted rules for the calling by the Economic and Social Council, under Article 62, paragraph 4, of the Charter, of international conferences of States.

9. At its fifth session, the General Assembly, by resolution 377 A (V) of 3 November 1950, adopted several

amendments and additions to its rules of procedure relating to the holding of emergency special sessions; by that resolution, the Assembly decided:

(a) To add a paragraph

(b) To rule 8; (b) To add a paragraph (b) to rule 9;

(c) To insert a new sentence at the end of rule 10;

(d) To insert a new sentence at the end of rule 16;

(e) To insert a new sentence at the end of rule 19;

(f) To insert a new rule 65 [See Rule 63 of the present rules of procedure].

10. At the same session, the General Assembly, by resolution 475 (V) of 1 November 1950, adopted a new rule 84A [See Rule 84 of the present rules of procedure] concerning the majority required for decisions of the Assembly on amendments to proposals relating to important questions and on parts of such proposals put to the vote separately.

11. At the same session, the General Assembly, by resolution 479 (V) of 12 December 1950, adopted rules for the calling by the Economic and Social Council, under Article 62, paragraph 4, of the Charter, of non-governmental conferences.

12. At its sixth session, the General Assembly, by resolution 597 (VI) of 20 December 1951, established the Special Committee for the Consideration of the Methods and Procedures of the General Assembly for Dealing with Legal and Drafting Questions, consisting of 15 Member States.

13. At its seventh session, the General Assembly considered the report of the Special Committee for the Consideration of the Methods and Procedures of the

General Assembly for Dealing with Legal and Drafting Questions [See Official Records of the General Assembly, Seventh Session, Annexes, agenda item 53, document A/2174] and, by resolution 684 (VII) of 6 November 1952, adopted certain recommendations contained in that report; the resolution also provided that:

(a) The terms of these recommendations should be embodied as an annex to the rules of procedure;

(b) The said annex should also reproduce paragraphs 19, 20, 29, 30 and 35 to 39 of the report of the Special Committee. The texts of the recommendations and the specified parts of the report of the Special Committee are reproduced in annex II.

14. At the same session, the General Assembly, by resolution 689 A (VII) of 21 December 1952, established the Special Committee on Measures to Limit the Duration of Regular Sessions of the General Assembly, consisting of 15 Member States. By resolution 689 B (VII) of the same date, the Assembly adopted an amendment to rule 2 whereby the Assembly would, at the beginning of each session, fix "a closing date for the session" rather than "a target date for the closing of the session".

15. At its eighth session, the General Assembly considered the report of the Special Committee on Measures to Limit the Duration of Regular Sessions of the General Assembly [See Official Records of the General Assembly, Eighth Session, Annexes, agenda item 54, document A/2402] and, by resolution 791 (VIII) of 23 October 1953, decided:

(a) To amend rules 38 and 39, relating to the composition of the General Committee;

(b) To amend rule 98 [See Rule 99 of the present rules

of procedure], relating to priorities in the consideration of items in the Main Committees.

16. At its ninth session, the General Assembly, by resolution 844 (IX) of 11 October 1954, adopted six special rules designed to govern its procedure for the examination of reports and petitions relating to the Territory of South West Africa [By resolution 2372 (XXII) of 12 June 1968, the General Assembly decided that "South West Africa" would be known as "Namibia". See paragraph 42 below].

17. At its eleventh session, the General Assembly, at the 577th plenary meeting on 15 November 1956, decided:

(a) To establish an eighth vice-presidency of the Assembly;

(b) To change the name of the "Ad Hoc Political Committee" to "Special Political Committee" and to confer a permanent character or that Committee.

At the same session, the General Assembly, by resolution 1104 (XI) of 18 December 1956, adopted consequential amendments to rules 31, 38, 39 and 101[See Rule 98 of the present rules of procedure].

18. At its twelfth session, the General Assembly, by resolution 1192 (XII) of 12 December 1957, decided to increase the number of Vice-Presidents of the Assembly from 8 to 13 and adopted consequential amendments to rules 31 and 38. In an annex to the resolution, the General Assembly approved the pattern according to which the Vice-Presidents should be elected.

19. At its sixteenth session, the General Assembly, by resolution 1659 (XVI) of 28 November 1961, decided to increase the membership of the Advisory Committee on Administrative and Budgetary Questions from 9 to 12 and adopted consequential amendments to rules 156

and 157 [See Rules 155 and 156 of the present rules of procedure].

20. At its seventeenth session, the General Assembly, at the 1162nd plenary meeting on 30 October 1962, established the Ad Hoc Committee on the Improvement of the Methods of Work of the General Assembly, consisting of 18 members. By resolution 1845 (XVII) of 19 December 1962, the Assembly decided to continue the Ad Hoc Committee.

21. At its eighteenth session, the General Assembly considered the report of the Ad Hoc Committee on the Improvement of the Methods of Work of the General Assembly [See Official Records of the General Assembly, Eighteenth Session, Annexes, agenda item 25, document A/5423] and, by resolution 1898 (XVIII) of 11 November 1963, took note of the observations contained in that report and approved the recommendations submitted by the Committee. The text of the resolution is reproduced in annex III.

22. At the same session, the General Assembly, by resolution 1990 (XVIII) of 17 December 1963, decided to increase the number of Vice-Presidents of the Assembly from 13 to 17 and adopted consequential amendments to rules 31 and 38. In an annex to the resolution, the Assembly approved the pattern according to which the President of the Assembly, the 17 Vice-Presidents of the Assembly and the 7 Chairmen of the Main Committees should be elected.

23. At its twentieth session, the General Assembly, by resolution 2046 (XX) of 8 December 1965, following the entry into force of the amendments to Articles 23, 27 and 61 of the Charter, amended its rules of procedure as follows:

(a) In rule 8 (b), the word "seven" was replaced by the word "nine";

(b) In rule 143 [See Rule 142 of the present rules of procedure], the word "three" was replaced by the word "five";

(c) In rule 146 [See Rule 145 of the present rules of procedure], the word "six" was replaced by the word "nine".

The pattern for the election of the non-permanent members of the Security Council is reproduced in a footnote to rule 142.

24. At its twenty-second session, the General Assembly, by resolution 2323 (XXII) of 16 December 1967, decided to amend rules 89 and 128 [See Rules 87 and 127 of the present rules of procedure] by adding to each of these rules a new paragraph (b) to take into account the installation of mechanical means of voting.

25. At the same session, the General Assembly, at the 1629th plenary meeting on 13 December 1967, took note of a correction to the French version of rule 15 [See Official Records of the General Assembly, Twenty-second Session. Annexes, agenda item 8, document A/BUR/169] whereby the words "caractère d'importance ou d'urgence" in the first sentence of that rule were replaced by the words "caractère d'importance et d'urgence".

26. At its twenty-third session, the General Assembly, by resolution 2390 (XXIII) of 25 November 1968, decided to increase the membership of the Committee on Contributions from 10 to 12 and adopted a consequential amendment to rule 159 [See Rule 158 of the present rules of procedure].

27. At the same session, the General Assembly, by resolution 2479 (XXIII) of 21 December 1968, decided to include Russian among its working languages and to amend accordingly rule 51.

28. At its twenty-fourth session, the General Assembly, by resolution 2553 (XXIV) of 12 December 1969, adopted amendments to rules 52, 53 and 55 [See paragraph 34 above] consequent upon the amendment to rule 51 adopted at the twenty-third session.

29. At its twenty-fifth session, the General Assembly, by resolution 2632 (XXV) of 9 November 1970, established the Special Committee on the Rationalization of the Procedures and Organization of the General Assembly, consisting of 31 Member States.

30. At its twenty-sixth session, the General Assembly considered the report of the Special Committee on the Rationalization of the Procedures and Organization of the General Assembly [See Official Records of the General Assembly, Twenty-sixth Session, Supplement No. 26 (A/8426)] and, by resolution 2837 (XXVI) of 17 December 1971, decided:

(a) To amend rule 60 [See Rule 58 of the present rules of procedure] to reflect the practice of the Assembly and its committees regarding the records and sound recordings of meetings;

(b) To amend rules 69 and 110 [See Rules 67 and 108 of the present rules of procedure] to authorize the presiding officer to declare a meeting open and permit the debate to proceed when at least one third of the members of the Assembly or one quarter of the members of a committee are present;

(c) To amend rules 74 and 115 [See Rules 72 and 114 of

the present rules of procedure] to permit no more than two representatives to speak in favour, and two against, a proposal to limit the time to be allowed to each speaker or the number of times each representative may speak on any question;

(d) To amend rule 100 to include in it more detailed provisions relating to the organization of work of the Main Committees, and to renumber it rule 101[See Rule 99 of the present rules of procedure] (former rule 101 became rule 100 [See Rule 98 of the present rules of procedure]);

(e) To amend rule 105 [See Rule 103 of the present rules of procedure] to provide that:

(i) Each Main Committee shall elect a Chairman, two Vice-Chairmen and a Rapporteur;

(ii) Each other committee shall elect a Chairman, one or more Vice-Chairmen and a Rapporteur;

(iii) Elections shall be held by secret ballot unless the committee decides otherwise in an election where only one candidate is standing;

(iv) The nomination of each candidate shall be limited to one speaker, after which the committee shall immediately proceed to the election and to adopt consequential amendments to rules 39 and l07[See Rule 105 of the present rules of procedure];

(f) To insert a new rule 112 [See Rule 110 of the present rules of procedure], relating to congratulations to the officers of Main Committees, and to renumber accordingly the existing rules 112 to 164 [See Rules 111 to 163 of the present rules of procedure].

By resolution 2837 (XXVI), the General Assembly also

approved the conclusions of the Special Committee and decided that they should be annexed to the rules of procedure; these conclusions are reproduced in annex IV. In one of the recommendations [See Resolution 2837 (XXVI), annex II, para. 128], the Secretary-General was requested to undertake a comparative study of the versions of the rules of procedure in the various official languages in order to ensure their concordance; this request was complied with and the relevant editing changes were incorporated in the rules.

31. At the same session, the General Assembly, by resolution 2798 (XXVI) of 13 December 1971, decided to increase the membership of the Advisory Committee on Administrative and Budgetary Questions from 12 to 13 and adopted a consequential amendment to rule 157 [See Rule 155 of the present rules of procedure].

32. At the same session, the General Assembly, by resolution 2847 (XXVI) of 20 December 1971, decided to amend Article 61 of the Charter to increase from 27 to 54 the number of members of the Economic and Social Council. By that resolution, the Assembly also decided that, upon the entry into force of the amendment to the Charter, the word "nine" in rule 147 [See Rule 145 of the present rules of procedure] would be replaced by the word "eighteen". The amendment to the Charter entered into force on 24 September 1973. The pattern for the election of the members of the Economic and Social Council, as set forth in resolution 2847 (XXVI), is reproduced in a footnote to rule 145.

33. At its twenty-seventh session, the General Assembly, by resolution 2913 (XXVII) of 9 November 1972, decided to increase the membership of the Committee on Contributions from 12 to 13 and adopted a

consequential amendment to rule 160 [See Rule 158 of the present rules of procedure].

34. At its twenty-eighth session, the General Assembly, by resolutions 3189 (XXVIII) and 3190 (XXVIII) of 18 December 1973, decided:

(a) To include Chinese among the working languages of the Assembly, its committees and its subcommittees;

(b) To include Arabic among the official and the working languages of the Assembly and its Main Committees.

By resolution 3191 (XXVIII) of 18 December 1973, the Assembly adopted consequential amendments to its rules of procedure, whereby rules 51 to 59 were replaced by new rules 51 to 57, and rules 60 to 165 were renumbered accordingly.

35. At its thirty-first session, the General Assembly, by resolution 31/95 of 14 December 1976, decided to increase the membership of the Committee on Contributions from 13 to 18 and, by resolution 31/96 of the same date, adopted a consequential amendment to rule 158.

36. At its thirty-second session, the General Assembly, by resolution 32/103 of 14 December 1977, decided to increase the membership of the Advisory Committee on Administrative and Budgetary Questions from 13 to 16 and adopted a consequential amendment to rule 155. By the same resolution, the Assembly also decided:

(a) To adopt an amendment to rule 156 whereby the members of the Advisory Committee would serve for a period of three years corresponding to "three calendar years" rather than "three financial years, as defined in the Financial Regulations of the United Nations";

(b) To amend rule 157 to take into account, inter alia, the biennial presentation of the budget.

37. At its thirty-third session, the General Assembly, by resolution 33/12 of 3 November 1978, adopted an amendment to rule 159 whereby the members of the Committee on Contributions would serve for a period of three years corresponding to "three calendar years" rather than "three financial years, as defined in the Financial Regulations of the United Nations".

38. At the same session, the General Assembly, by resolution 33/138 of 19 December 1978, decided to increase the number of Vice-Presidents of the Assembly from 17 to 21 and adopted consequential amendments to rules 30 and 38. In an annex to the resolution, which replaced the annex to resolution 1990 (XVIII) [See paragraph 22 above], the Assembly approved the pattern according to which the President of the Assembly, the 21 Vice-Presidents of the Assembly and the 7 Chairmen of the Main Committees should be elected; the text of that annex is reproduced in a footnote to rule 30.

39. At its thirty-fourth session, the General Assembly, by decision 34/401 of 21 September, 25 October, 29 November and 12 December 1979, adopted a number of provisions concerning the rationalization of the procedures and organization of the Assembly. Sections I to V of the decision are reproduced in annex V.

40. At its thirty-fifth session, the General Assembly, by resolutions 35/219 A and B of 17 December 1980, decided to include Arabic among the official and working languages of the subsidiary organs of the Assembly, no later than 1 January 1982, and adopted consequential amendments to rules 51, 52, 54 and 56.

41. At its thirty-ninth session, the General Assembly, by

resolution 39/88 B of 13 December 1984, approved the conclusions of the Special Committee on the Charter of the United Nations and on the Strengthening of the Role of the Organization concerning the rationalization of the procedures of the Assembly and decided that they should be annexed to the rules of procedure; these conclusions are reproduced in annex VI.

42. As a result of the accession of Namibia (formerly the Territory of South West Africa) to independence on 21 March 1990, annex III to the rules of procedure (A/520/Rev.15), entitled "Procedure for the examination of reports and petitions relating to the Territory of South West Africa", is no longer applicable and has been removed. Subsequent annexes have been renumbered accordingly.

43. At its forty-fifth session, the General Assembly, by its resolution 45/45 of 28 November 1990, approved the conclusions of the Special Committee on the Charter of the United Nations and on the Strengthening of the Role of the Organization concerning the rationalization of existing United Nations procedures, and decided that they should be reproduced as an annex to its rules of procedure. These conclusions are reproduced in annex VII.

44. At its forty-seventh session, the General Assembly, by its resolution 47/233 of 17 August 1993, decided to rationalize the structure of the Main Committees of the Assembly and to amend accordingly rules 31 [See Rule 30 of the present rules of procedure], 38 and 98 of its rules of procedure.

45. At its forty-eighth session, the General Assembly, by its resolution 48/264 of 29 July 1994, adopted the Guidelines on the Rationalization of the Agenda of the

General Assembly, set forth in annex I to the resolution, and decided that they should be annexed to its rules of procedure. The Guidelines are reproduced in annex VIII. By the same resolution, the Assembly approved the pattern of election of the six Chairmen of the Main Committees, set forth in annex II to the resolution. The text of that annex, which replaced paragraph 4 of the annex to resolution 33/138 of 19 December 1978, is reproduced in a footnote to rule 30.

46. At its fifty-second session, the General Assembly, by its resolution 52/163 of 15 December 1997, decided to amend the first sentence of rule 103 of the rules of procedure to increase the number of Vice-Chairmen of each Main Committee from two to three, as from the fifty-third session.

47. At its fifty-fifth session, the General Assembly, by its resolution 55/14 of 3 November 2000, amended rule 1 of the rules of procedure whereby the Assembly would meet every year in regular session commencing "on the Tuesday following the second Monday in September".

48. At its fifty-sixth session, the General Assembly, by its resolution 56/509 of 8 July 2002, decided:

(a) To amend rule 30 to allow the Assembly to elect a President and twenty-one Vice-Presidents at least three months before the opening of the session over which they are to preside;

(b) To amend rule 31 so that if at the opening of a session of the Assembly, the President for that session has not yet been elected, the President of the previous session, or the chairman of that delegation from which the President of the previous session was elected, would preside until the Assembly has elected a President;

(c) To amend paragraph (a) of rule 99 to allow all the Main Committees, at least three months before the opening of the session, to elect a Chairman and elections of the other officers provided for in rule 103 to be held at the latest by the end of the first week of the session.

49. At its fifty-seventh session, the General Assembly, by its resolution 57/301 of 13 March 2003, amended rule 1 of the rules of procedure whereby the Assembly would meet every year in regular session commencing on the Tuesday of the third week in September, counting from the first week that contains at least one working day.

50. At the same session, the General Assembly, by its resolution 57/301 of 13 March 2003, decided to change the opening date and length of the general debate and also decided to annex paragraph 2 of the resolution to the rules of procedure. The paragraph is reproduced in annex IX.

51. The present revised edition of the rules of procedure embodies all the amendments adopted by the General Assembly during the period up to and including its sixty-first session and incorporates the technical corrections in document A/520/Rev.16/Corr.1.

52. The previous versions of the rules of procedure and of the amendments and corrigenda thereto have been issued under the following symbols:

- December 1947: A/520
- June 1948: A/520/Corr.1 (French only)
- January 1950: A/520/Rev.1
- January 1951: A/520/Rev 2
- July 1954: A/520/Rev.3
- March 1956: A/520/Rev.4
- September 1957: A/520/Rev.5 (formerly A/3660)

- January 1958: A/520/Rev.5/Corr.1 (formerly A/3660/Corr.1)
- February 1961: A/520/Rev.6 (formerly A/4700)
- February 1962: A/520/Rev 6/Corr.1 (formerly A/4700/Corr.1)
- June 1964: A/520/Rev.7
- March 1966: A/520/Rev.8
- January 1968: A/520/Rev.9
- April 1969: A/520/Rev.9/Corr.1
- July 1970: A/520/Rev.10
- May 1972: A/520/Rev.11
- November 1973: A/520/Rev.11/Amend.1
- February 1974: A/520/Rev.12
- January 1977: A/520/Rev.12/Amend.1
- March 1978: A/520/Rev.12/Amend.2
- March 1979: A/520/Rev.13
- March 1982: A/520/Rev.14
- May 1985: A/520/Rev.15
- August 1991: A/520/Rev.15/Amend.1
- October 1993: A/520/Rev.15/Amend.2
- September 2006: A/520/Rev.16
- September 2007: A/520/Rev.16/Corr 1

I. Sessions

Regular Sessions

Opening date

Rule 1

[based directly on a provision of the Charter (Art. 20), see introduction paras. 46 and 48]

The General Assembly shall meet every year in regular session commencing on the Tuesday of the third week in September, counting from the first week that contains at least one working day.

Closing date

Rule 2

On the recommendation of the General Committee, the General Assembly shall, at the beginning of each session, fix a closing date for the session.

Place of Meeting

Rule 3

The General Assembly shall meet at the Headquarters of the United Nations unless convened elsewhere in pursuance of a decision taken at a previous session or at the request of a majority of the Members of the United Nations.

Rule 4

Any Member of the United Nations may, at least one hundred and twenty days before the date fixed for the opening of a regular session, request that the session be held elsewhere than at the Headquarters of the United Nations. The Secretary-General shall immediately communicate the request, together with his recommendations, to the other Members of the United Nations. If within thirty days of the date of this communication a majority of the Members concur in the request, the session shall be held accordingly.

Notification of Session

Rule 5

The Secretary-General shall notify the Members of the

United Nations, at least sixty days in advance, of the opening of a regular session.

Temporary Adjournment of Session

Rule 6

The General Assembly may decide at any session to adjourn temporarily and resume its meetings at a later date.

Special Sessions

Summoning by the General Assembly

Rule 7

[based directly on a provision of the Charter (Art. 20)]

The General Assembly may fix a date for a special session.

Summoning at the request of the Security Council or Members

Rule 8

(a) Special sessions of the General Assembly shall be convened within fifteen days of the receipt by the Secretary-General of a request for such a session from the Security Council or from a majority of the Members of the United Nations or of the concurrence of a majority of Members as provided in rule 9.

(b) Emergency special sessions pursuant to General Assembly resolution 377 A (V) shall be convened within twenty-four hours of the receipt by the Secretary-General of a request for such a session from the Security Council, on the vote of any nine members thereof, or of a request from a majority of the Members of the United Nations expressed by vote in the Interim Committee or otherwise, or of the concurrence of a majority of Members as provided in rule 9.

Request by Members

Rule 9

(a) Any Member of the United Nations may request the Secretary-General to convene a special session of the General Assembly. The Secretary-General shall immediately inform the other Members of the request and inquire whether they concur in it. If within thirty days of the date of the communication of the Secretary-General a majority of the Members concur in the request, a special session of the General Assembly shall be convened in accordance with rule 8.

(b) This rule shall apply also to a request by any Member of the United Nations for an emergency special session pursuant to resolution 377 A (V). In such a case, the Secretary-General shall communicate with the other Members by the most expeditious means of communication available.

Notification of session

Rule 10

The Secretary-General shall notify the Members of the United Nations, at least fourteen days in advance, of the opening of a special session convened at the request of the Security Council, and at least ten days in advance in the case of a session convened at the request of a majority of the Members or upon the concurrence of a majority in the request of any Member. In the case of an emergency special session convened pursuant to rule 8 (b), the Secretary-General shall notify Members at least twelve hours before the opening of the session.

Regular and Special Sessions

Notification to other bodies

Rule 11

Copies of the notice convening each session of the

General Assembly shall be addressed to all other principal organs of the United Nations and to the specialized agencies referred to in Article 57, paragraph 2, of the Charter.

II. Agenda

Regular Sessions

Provisional agenda

Rule 12

The provisional agenda for a regular session shall be drawn up by the Secretary-General and communicated to the Members of the United Nations at least sixty days before the opening of the session.

Rule 13

The provisional agenda of a regular session shall include:

(a) The report of the Secretary-General on the work of the Organization;

(b) Reports from the Security Council, the Economic and Social Council, the Trusteeship Council, the International Court of Justice, the subsidiary organs of the General Assembly and the specialized agencies (where such reports are called for under agreements entered into);

(c) All items the inclusion of which has been ordered by the General Assembly at a previous session;

(d) All items proposed by the other principal organs of the United Nations;

(e) All items proposed by any Member of the United Nations [See annex IV, para. 18, and annex VI, para. 2];

(f) All items pertaining to the budget for the next financial year and the report on the accounts for the last financial year;

(g) All items which the Secretary-General deems it

necessary to put before the General Assembly;

(h) All items proposed under Article 35, paragraph 2, of the Charter by States not Members of the United Nations.

Supplementary items

Rule 14

Any Member or principal organ of the United Nations or the Secretary-General may, at least thirty days before the date fixed for the opening of a regular session, request the inclusion of supplementary items in the agenda [See annex IV, para. 18, and annex VI, para. 2]. Such items shall be placed on a supplementary list, which shall be communicated to Members at least twenty days before the opening of the session.

Additional items

Rule 15

Additional items of an important and urgent character, proposed for inclusion in the agenda less than thirty days before the opening of a regular session or during a regular session, may be placed on the agenda if the General Assembly so decides by a majority of the members present and voting.

No additional item may, unless the General Assembly decides otherwise by a two-thirds majority of the members present and voting, be considered until seven days have elapsed since it was placed on the agenda and until a committee has reported upon the question concerned.

Special Sessions

Provisional agenda

Rule 16

The provisional agenda of a special session convened

at the request of the Security Council shall be communicated to the Members of the United Nations at least fourteen days before the opening of the session.

The provisional agenda of a special session convened at the request of a majority of the Members, or upon the concurrence of a majority in the request of any Member, shall be communicated at least ten days before the opening of the session. The provisional agenda of an emergency special session shall be communicated to Members simultaneously with the communication convening the session.

Rule 17

The provisional agenda for a special session shall consist only of those items proposed for consideration in the request for the holding of the session.

Supplementary items

Rule 18

Any Member or principal organ of the United Nations or the Secretary-General may, at least four days before the date fixed for the opening of a special session, request the inclusion of supplementary items in the agenda. Such items shall be placed on a supplementary list, which shall be communicated to Members as soon as possible.

Additional items

Rule 19

During a special session, items on the supplementary list and additional items may be added to the agenda by a two-thirds majority of the members present and voting. During an emergency special session, additional items concerning the matters dealt with in resolution 377 A (V) may be added to the agenda by a two-thirds majority of the members present and voting.

Regular and Special Sessions

Explanatory memorandum

Rule 20

Any item proposed for inclusion in the agenda shall be accompanied by an explanatory memorandum and, if possible, by basic documents or by a draft resolution.

Adoption of the agenda

Rule 21

At each session the provisional agenda and the supplementary list, together with the report of the General Committee thereon, shall be submitted to the General Assembly for approval as soon as possible after the opening of the session.

Amendment and deletion of items

Rule 22

Items on the agenda may be amended or deleted by the General Assembly by a majority of the members present and voting.

Debate on inclusion of items

Rule 23

Debate on the inclusion of an item in the agenda, when that item has been recommended for inclusion by the General Committee, shall be limited to three speakers in favour of, and three against, the inclusion. The President may limit the time to be allowed to speakers under this rule.

Modification of the allocation of expenses

Rule 24

No proposal for a modification of the allocation of expenses for the time being in force shall be placed on the agenda unless it has been communicated to the Members of the United Nations at least ninety days before the opening of the session.

III. Delegations

Composition

Rule 25

The delegation of a Member shall consist of not more than five representatives and five alternate representatives and as many advisers, technical advisers, experts and persons of similar status as may be required by the delegation.

Alternates

Rule 26

An alternate representative may act as a representative upon designation by the chairman of the delegation.

IV. Credentials

Submission of credentials

Rule 27

The credentials of representatives and the names of members of a delegation shall be submitted to the Secretary-General if possible not less than one week before the opening of the session. The credentials shall be issued either by the Head of the State or Government or by the Minister for Foreign Affairs.

Credentials Committee

Rule 28

A Credentials Committee shall be appointed at the beginning of each session. It shall consist of nine members, who shall be appointed by the General Assembly on the proposal of the President. The Committee shall elect its own officers. It shall examine the credentials of representatives and report without delay.

Provisional admission to a session

Rule 29

Any representative to whose admission a Member has made objection shall be seated provisionally with the same rights as other representatives until the Credentials Committee has reported and the General Assembly has given its decision.

V. President and Vice-Presidents

Elections

Rule 30

Unless the General Assembly decides otherwise, the General Assembly shall elect a President and twenty-one Vice-Presidents [In the annex to resolution 33/138 of 19 December 1978, the General Assembly decided as follows:

"1. In the election of the President of the General Assembly, regard shall be had for equitable geographical rotation of this office among the regions mentioned in paragraph 4 below.

"2. The twenty-one Vice-Presidents of the General Assembly shall be elected according to the following pattern, subject to paragraph 3 below: "(a) Six representatives from African States;"

(b) Five representatives from Asian States; "(c) One representative from an Eastern European State; "(d) Three representatives from Latin American States; "(e) Two representatives from Western European or other States; "(f) Five representatives from the permanent members of the Security Council ".

3. The election of the President of the General Assembly will, however, have the effect of reducing by one the number of vice-presidencies allocated to the region from which the President is elected. In annex II to its resolution 48/264 of 29 July 1994, the General Assembly decided to replace paragraph 4 of the annex to resolution 33/138 to read as follows:

"4. The six Chairmen of the Main Committees shall be elected according to the following pattern: "(a) One representative from an African State; "(b) One representative from an Asian State; "(c) One representative from an Eastern European State; "(d) One representative from a Latin American or Caribbean State; "(e) One representative from a Western European or other State; "(f) The sixth chairmanship shall rotate over a period of twenty sessions according to the following pattern:

i. One representative from an African State;
ii. One representative from an Asian State;
iii. One representative from a Latin American or Caribbean State;
iv. One representative from an African State;
v. One representative from an Asian State;
vi. One representative from an African State;
vii. One representative from a Latin American or Caribbean State;

viii. One representative from an Asian State;

ix. One representative from an African State;

x. One representative from an Asian State;

xi. One representative from a Latin American or Caribbean State;

xii. One representative from an African State;

xiii. One representative from an Asian State;

xiv. One representative from an African State;

xv. One representative from a Latin American or Caribbean State;

xvi. One representative from an Asian State;

xvii. One representative from an African State;

xviii. One representative from an Asian State;

xix. One representative from a Latin American or Caribbean State;

xx. One representative from an African State at least three months before the opening of the session over which they are to preside. The President and the Vice-Presidents so elected will assume their functions only at the beginning of the session for which they are elected and shall hold office until the close of that session [Rule based directly on a provision of the Charter (Art. 21, second sentence)]. The Vice-Presidents shall be elected after the election of the Chairmen of the six Main Committees referred to in rule 98, in such a way as to ensure the representative character of the General Committee.

Temporary President

Rule 31

If, at the opening of a session of the General Assembly,

the President for that session has not yet been elected, in accordance with rule 30 above, the President of the previous session, or the chairman of that delegation from which the President of the previous session was elected, shall preside until the Assembly has elected a President.

Acting President

Rule 32

If the President finds it necessary to be absent during a meeting or any part thereof, he shall designate one of the Vice-Presidents to take his place.

Rule 33

A Vice-President acting as President shall have the same powers and duties as the President.

Replacement of the President

Rule 34

If the President is unable to perform his functions, a new President shall be elected for the unexpired term.

General powers of the President

Rule 35

IV, paras. 39 and 67, annex V, para. 3, and annex VI, para 7]

In addition to exercising the powers conferred upon him elsewhere by these rules, the President shall declare the opening and closing of each plenary meeting of the session, direct the discussions in plenary meeting, ensure observance of these rules, accord the right to speak, put questions and announce decisions. He shall rule on points of order and, subject to these rules, shall have complete control of the proceedings at any meeting and over the maintenance of order thereat.

The President may, in the course of the discussion of an item, propose to the General Assembly the limitation of the time to be allowed to speakers, the limitation of the number of times each representative may speak, the closure of the list of speakers or the closure of the debate. He may also propose the suspension or the adjournment of the meeting or the adjournment of the debate on the item under discussion.

Rule 36

The President, in the exercise of his functions, remains under the authority of the General Assembly.

The President shall not vote

Rule 37

The President, or a Vice-President acting as President, shall not vote but shall designate another member of his delegation to vote in his place.

VI. General Committee

Composition

Rule 38

The General Committee shall comprise the President of the General Assembly, who shall preside, the twenty-one Vice-Presidents and the Chairmen of the six Main Committees. No two members of the General Committee shall be members of the same delegation, and it shall be so constituted as to ensure its representative character. Chairmen of other committees upon which all Members have the right to be represented and which are established by the General

Assembly to meet during the session shall be entitled to attend meetings of the General Committee and may participate without vote in the discussions.

Substitute members

Rule 39

If a Vice-President of the General Assembly finds it necessary to be absent during a meeting of the General Committee, he may designate a member of his delegation to take his place. The Chairman of a Main Committee shall, in case of absence, designate one of the Vice-Chairmen of the Committee to take his place. A Vice-Chairman shall not have the right to vote if he is of the same delegation as another member of the General Committee.

Functions

Rule 40

The General Committee shall, at the beginning of each session, consider the provisional agenda, together with the supplementary list, and shall make recommendations to the General Assembly, with regard to each item proposed, concerning its inclusion in the agenda, the rejection of the request for inclusion or the inclusion of the item in the provisional agenda of a future session. It shall, in the same manner, examine requests for the inclusion of additional items in the agenda and shall make recommendations thereon to the General Assembly. In considering matters relating to the agenda of the General Assembly, the General Committee shall not discuss the substance of any item except insofar as this bears upon the question whether the General Committee should recommend the inclusion of the item in the agenda, the rejection of the request for inclusion or the inclusion of the item in the provisional agenda of a future session, and what priority should be accorded to an item the inclusion of which has been recommended.

Rule 41

The General Committee shall make recommendations to the General Assembly concerning the closing date of the session. It shall assist the President and the General Assembly in drawing up the agenda for each plenary meeting, in determining the priority of its items and in coordinating the proceedings of all committees of the Assembly. It shall assist the President in the general conduct of the work of the General Assembly which falls within the competence of the President. It shall not, however, decide any political question.

Rule 42

The General Committee shall meet periodically throughout each session to review the progress of the General Assembly and its committees and to make recommendations for furthering such progress. It shall also meet at such other times as the President deems necessary or upon the request of any other of its members.

Participation by members requesting the inclusion of items in the agenda

Rule 43

A member of the General Assembly which has no representative on the General Committee and which has requested the inclusion of an item in the agenda shall be entitled to attend any meeting of the General Committee at which its request is discussed and may participate, without vote, in the discussion of that item.

Revision of the form of resolutions

Rule 44

The General Committee may revise the resolutions adopted by the General Assembly, changing their form but not their substance. Any such changes shall be reported to the General Assembly for its consideration.

VII. Secretariat

Duties of the Secretary-General

Rule 45

The Secretary-General shall act in that capacity in all meetings of the General Assembly, its committees and its subcommittees. He may designate a member of the Secretariat to act in his place at these meetings.

Rule 46

The Secretary-General shall provide and direct the staff required by the General Assembly and any committees or subsidiary organs which it may establish.

Duties of the Secretariat

Rule 47

The Secretariat shall receive, translate, print and distribute documents, reports and resolutions of the General Assembly, its committees and its organs [See annex IV, para. 107, and annex V, paras. 25, 26 and 28-30]; interpret speeches made at the meetings; prepare, print and circulate the records of the session [See annex IV, para. 108]; have the custody and proper preservation of the documents in the archives of the General Assembly; distribute all documents of the Assembly to the Members of the United Nations, and, generally, perform all other work which the Assembly may require.

Report of the Secretary-General on the work of the Organization

Rule 48

The Secretary-General shall make an annual report, and such supplementary reports as are required, to the General Assembly on the work of the Organization [See introduction, para. 7; see also annex I, para. 20, annex III, para. (f), annex IV, paras. 13 and 14, annex V, para. 2, annex VI, para. 4 and annex VII, para. 5]. He shall communicate the annual report to the Members of the United Nations at least forty-five days before the opening of the session.

Notification under Article 12 of the Charter

Rule 49

The Secretary-General, with the consent of the Security Council, shall notify the General Assembly at each session of any matters relative to the maintenance of international peace and security which are being dealt with by the Security Council and shall similarly notify the General Assembly, or the Members of the United Nations if the General Assembly is not in session, immediately the Security Council ceases to deal with such matters.

Regulations concerning the Secretariat

Rule 50

The General Assembly shall establish regulations concerning the staff of the Secretariat [For the Staff Regulations of the United Nations, see ST/SGB/2007/4].

VIII. Languages

Official and working languages

Rule 51

[see introduction paras. 5, 27, 28, 34 and 40]

Arabic, Chinese, English, French, Russian and Spanish shall be both the official and the working languages of the General Assembly, its committees and its subcommittees.

Interpretation

Rule 52

Speeches made in any of the six languages of the General Assembly shall be interpreted into the other five languages.

Rule 53

Any representative may make a speech in a language other than the languages of the General Assembly. In this case, he shall himself provide for interpretation into one of the languages of the General Assembly or of the committee concerned. Interpretation into the other languages of the General Assembly or of the committee concerned by the interpreters of the Secretariat may be based on the interpretation given in the first such language.

Languages of verbatim and summary records

Rule 54

Verbatim or summary records shall be drawn up as soon as possible in the languages of the General Assembly.

Languages of the Journal of the United Nations

Rule 55

During the sessions of the General Assembly, the

Journal of the United Nations shall be published in the languages of the Assembly.

Languages of resolutions and other documents

Rule 56

All resolutions and other documents shall be published in the languages of the General Assembly.

Publications in languages other than the languages of the General Assembly

Rule 57

Documents of the General Assembly, its committees and its subcommittees shall, if the Assembly so decides, be published in any language other than the languages of the Assembly or of the committee concerned.

IX. Records

Records and sound recordings of meetings

Rule 58

(a) Verbatim records of the meetings of the General Assembly and of the Disarmament and International Security (First Committee) shall be drawn up by the Secretariat and submitted to those organs after approval by the presiding officer. The General Assembly shall decide upon the form of the records of the meetings of the other Main Committees and, if any, of the subsidiary organs and of special meetings and conferences. No organ of the General Assembly shall have both verbatim and summary records.

(b) Sound recordings of the meetings of the General Assembly and of the Main Committees shall be made by the Secretariat. Such recordings shall also be made of the proceedings of subsidiary organs and special meetings and conferences when they so decide.

Resolutions

Rule 59

Resolutions adopted by the General Assembly shall be communicated by the Secretary-General to the Members of the United Nations within fifteen days after the close of the session.

X. Public and Private Meetings of the General Assembly, its Committees and its Subcommittees

General principles

Rule 60

The meetings of the General Assembly and its Main Committees shall be held in public unless the organ concerned decides that exceptional circumstances require that the meeting be held in private. Meetings of other committees and subcommittees shall also be held in public unless the organ concerned decides otherwise.

Private meetings

Rule 61

All decisions of the General Assembly taken at a private meeting shall be announced at an early public meeting of the Assembly. At the close of each private meeting of the Main Committees, other committees and subcommittees, the Chairman may issue a communiqué through the Secretary-General.

XI. Minute of Silent Prayer or Meditation

Invitation to silent prayer or meditation

Rule 62

Immediately after the opening of the first plenary meeting and immediately preceding the closing of the final plenary meeting of each session of the General Assembly, the President shall invite the representatives to observe one minute of silence dedicated to prayer or meditation.

XII. Plenary Meetings

Conduct of Business

Emergency special sessions

Rule 63

Notwithstanding the provisions of any other rule and unless the General Assembly decides otherwise, the Assembly, in case of an emergency special session, shall convene in plenary meeting only and proceed directly to consider the item proposed for consideration in the request for the holding of the session, without previous reference to the General Committee or to any other committee; the President and Vice-Presidents for such emergency special sessions shall be, respectively, the chairmen of those delegations from which were elected the President and Vice-Presidents of the previous session.

Report of the Secretary-General

Rule 64

Proposals to refer any portion of the report of the Secretary-General to one of the Main Committees without debate shall be decided upon by the General Assembly without previous reference to the General Committee.

Reference to committees

Rule 65

The General Assembly shall not, unless it decides otherwise, make a final decision upon any item on the agenda until it has received the report of a committee on that item.

Discussion of reports of Main Committees

Rule 66

Discussion of a report of a Main Committee in a plenary meeting of the General Assembly shall take place if at least one third of the members present and voting at the plenary meeting consider such a discussion to be necessary. Any proposal to this effect shall not be debated but shall be immediately put to the vote.

Quorum

Rule 67

The President may declare a meeting open and permit the debate to proceed when at least one third of the members of the General Assembly are present. The presence of a majority of the members shall be required for any decision to be taken.

Speeches

Rule 68

No representative may address the General Assembly without having previously obtained the permission of the President. The President shall call upon speakers in the order in which they signify their desire to speak.

The President may call a speaker to order if his remarks are not relevant to the subject under discussion.

Precedence

Rule 69

The Chairman and the Rapporteur of a committee may be accorded precedence for the purpose of explaining the conclusions arrived at by their committee.

Statements by the Secretariat

Rule 70

The Secretary-General, or a member of the Secretariat designated by him as his representative, may at any time make either oral or written statements to the General Assembly concerning any question under consideration by it.

Points of order

Rule 71

During the discussion of any matter, a representative may rise to a point of order, and the point of order shall be immediately decided by the President in accordance with the rules of procedure. A representative may appeal against the ruling of the President. The appeal shall be immediately put to the vote, and the President's ruling shall stand unless overruled by a majority of the members present and voting. A representative rising to a point of order may not speak on the substance of the matter under discussion.

Time limit on speeches

Rule 72 [114]

The General Assembly may limit the time to be allowed to each speaker and the number of times each representative may speak on any question. Before a decision is taken, two representatives may speak in favour of, and two against, a proposal to set such limits. When the debate is limited and a representative exceeds his allotted time, the President shall call him to order without delay.

Closing of list of speakers, right of reply

Rule 73

During the course of a debate, the President may announce the list of speakers and, with the consent of the General Assembly, declare the list closed.

He may, however, accord the right of reply to any member if a speech delivered after he has declared the list closed makes this desirable.

Adjournment of debate

Rule 74

During the discussion of any matter, a representative may move the adjournment of the debate on the item under discussion. In addition to the proposer of the motion, two representatives may speak in favour of, and two against, the motion, after which the motion shall be immediately put to the vote.

The President may limit the time to be allowed to speakers under this rule.

Closure of debate

Rule 75

A representative may at any time move the closure of the debate on the item under discussion, whether or not any other representative has signified his wish to speak. Permission to speak on the closure of the debate shall be accorded only to two speakers opposing the closure, after which the motion shall be immediately put to the vote.

If the General Assembly is in favour of the closure, the President shall declare the closure of the debate. The President may limit the time to be allowed to speakers under this rule.

Suspension or adjournment of the meeting

Rule 76

During the discussion of any matter, a representative may move the suspension or the adjournment of the meeting. Such motions shall not be debated but shall be immediately put to the vote. The President may limit the time to be allowed to the speaker moving the suspension or adjournment of the meeting.

Order of procedural motions

Rule 77

Subject to rule 71, the motions indicated below shall have precedence in the following order over all other proposals or motions before the meeting:

(a) To suspend the meeting;

(b) To adjourn the meeting;

(c) To adjourn the debate on the item under discussion;

(d) To close the debate on the item under discussion.

Proposals and amendments

Rule 78

Proposals and amendments shall normally be submitted in writing to the Secretary-General, who shall circulate copies to the delegations.

As a general rule, no proposal shall be discussed or put to the vote at any meeting of the General Assembly unless copies of it have been circulated to all delegations not later than the day preceding the meeting.

The President may, however, permit the discussion and consideration of amendments, or of motions as to procedure, even though such amendments and motions have not been circulated or have only been circulated the same day.

Decisions on competence

Rule 79

Subject to rule 77, any motion calling for a decision on the competence of the General Assembly to adopt a proposal submitted to it shall be put to the vote before a vote is taken on the proposal in question.

Withdrawal of motions

Rule 80

A motion may be withdrawn by its proposer at any time before voting on it has commenced, provided that the motion has not been amended. A motion thus withdrawn may be reintroduced by any member.

Reconsideration of proposals

Rule 81

When a proposal has been adopted or rejected, it may not be reconsidered at the same session unless the General Assembly, by a two-thirds majority of the members present and voting, so decides. Permission to speak on a motion to reconsider shall be accorded only to two speakers opposing the motion, after which it shall be immediately put to the vote.

Voting

Voting rights

Rule 82

Each member of the General Assembly shall have one vote.

Two-thirds majority

Rule 83

Decisions of the General Assembly on important questions shall be made by a two-thirds majority of the members present and voting. These questions shall include: recommendations with respect to the maintenance of international peace and security, the election of the non-permanent members of the Security Council, the election of the members of the Economic and Social Council, the election of members of the Trusteeship Council in accordance with paragraph 1c of Article 86 of the Charter, the admission of new Members to the United Nations, the suspension of the rights an d privileges of membership, the expulsion of Members, questions relating to the operation of the trusteeship system, and budgetary questions.

Rule 84

Decisions of the General Assembly on amendments to proposals relating to important questions, and on parts of such proposals put to the vote separately, shall be made by a two-thirds majority of the members present and voting.

Simple majority

Rule 85

Decisions of the General Assembly on questions other than those provided for in rule 83, including the determination of additional categories of questions to be decided by a two-thirds majority, shall be made by a majority of the members present and voting.

Meaning of the phrase "members present and voting"

Rule 86

For the purposes of these rules, the phrase "members

present and voting" means members casting an affirmative or negative vote. Members which abstain from voting are considered as not voting.

Method of voting

Rule 87

(a) The General Assembly shall normally vote by show of hands or by standing, but any representative may request a roll-call. The roll-call shall be taken in the English alphabetical order of the names of the members, beginning with the member whose name is drawn by lot by the President. The name of each member shall be called in any roll-call, and one of its representatives shall reply "yes", "no" or "abstention". The result of the voting shall be inserted in the record in the English alphabetical order of the names of the members.

(b) When the General Assembly votes by mechanical means, a non-recorded vote shall replace a vote by show of hands or by standing and a recorded vote shall replace a roll-call vote. Any representative may request a recorded vote. In the case of a recorded vote, the General Assembly shall, unless a representative requests otherwise, dispense with the procedure of calling out the names of the members; nevertheless, the result of the voting shall be inserted in the record in the same manner as that of a roll-call vote.

Conduct during voting

Rule 88

After the President has announced the beginning of voting, no representative shall interrupt the voting except on a point of order in connection with the actual conduct of the voting. The President may permit members to explain their votes, either before or after the voting, except when the vote is taken by secret ballot. The President may limit the time to be allowed for such explanations. The President shall not permit the proposer of a proposal or of an amendment to explain his vote on his own proposal or amendment.

Division of proposals and amendments

Rule 89

A representative may move that parts of a proposal or of an amendment should be voted on separately. If objection is made to the request for division, the motion for division shall be voted upon. Permission to speak on the motion for division shall be given only to two speakers in favour and two speakers against. If the motion for division is carried, those parts of the proposal or of the amendment which are approved shall then be put to the vote as a whole. If all operative parts of the proposal or of the amendment have been rejected, the proposal or the amendment shall be considered to have been rejected as a whole.

Voting on amendments

Rule 90

When an amendment is moved to a proposal, the amendment shall be voted on first. When two or more amendments are moved to a proposal, the General Assembly shall first vote on the amendment furthest removed in substance from the original proposal and then on the amendment next furthest removed therefrom, and so on until all the amendments have been put to the vote. Where, however, the adoption of one amendment necessarily implies the rejection of another amendment, the latter amendment shall not be put to the vote. If one or more amendments are adopted, the amended proposal shall then be voted upon. A motion is considered an amendment to a proposal if it merely adds to, deletes from or revises part of the proposal.

Voting on proposals

Rule 91

If two or more proposals relate to the same question, the General Assembly shall, unless it decides otherwise, vote on the proposals in the order in which they have been submitted. The General Assembly may, after each vote on a proposal, decide whether to vote on the next proposal.

Elections

Rule 92

All elections shall be held by secret ballot. There shall be no nominations.

Rule 93

When only one person or Member is to be elected and no candidate obtains in the first ballot the majority required, a second ballot shall be taken, which shall be restricted to the two candidates obtaining the largest number of votes. If in the second ballot the votes are equally divided, and a majority is required, the President shall decide between the candidates by drawing lots. If a two-thirds majority is required, the balloting shall be continued until one candidate secures two thirds of the votes cast; provided that, after the third inconclusive ballot, votes may be cast for any eligible person or Member. If three such unrestricted ballots are inconclusive, the next three ballots shall be restricted to the two candidates who obtained the greatest number of votes in the third of the unrestricted ballots, and the following three ballots thereafter shall be unrestricted, and so on until a person or Member is elected. These provisions shall not prejudice the application of rules 143, 144, 146 and 148.

Rule 94

When two or more elective places are to be filled at one time under the same conditions, those candidates obtaining in the first ballot the majority required shall be elected. If the number of candidates obtaining such majority is less than the number of persons or Members to be elected, there shall be additional ballots to fill the remaining places, the voting being restricted to the candidates obtaining the greatest number of votes in the previous ballot to a number not more than twice the places remaining to be filled; provided that, after the third inconclusive ballot, votes may be cast for any eligible person or Member. If three such unrestricted ballots are inconclusive, the next three ballots shall be restricted to the candidates who obtained the greatest number of votes in the third of the unrestricted ballots, to a number not more than twice the places remaining to be filled, and the following three ballots thereafter shall be unrestricted, and so on until all the places have been filled. These provisions shall not prejudice the application of rules 143, 144, 146 and 148.

Equally divided votes

Rule 95

If a vote is equally divided on matters other than elections, a second vote shall be taken at a subsequent meeting which shall be held within forty-eight hours of the first vote; and it shall be expressly mentioned in the agenda that a second vote will be taken on the matter in question. If this vote also results in equality, the proposal shall be regarded as rejected.

XIII. Committees

Establishment, Officers, Organization of Work

Establishment of committees

Rule 96

The General Assembly may establish such committees as it deems necessary for the performance of its functions.

Categories of subjects

Rule 97

Items relating to the same category of subjects shall be referred to the committee or committees dealing with that category of subjects. Committees shall not introduce new items on their own initiative.

Main Committees

Rule 98

The Main Committees of the General Assembly are the following:

(a) Disarmament and International Security Committee (First Committee);

(b) Special Political and Decolonization Committee (Fourth Committee);

(c) Economic and Financial Committee (Second Committee);

(d) Social, Humanitarian and Cultural Committee (Third Committee);

(e) Administrative and Budgetary Committee (Fifth Committee);

(f) Legal Committee (Sixth Committee).

Organization of work

Rule 99

(a) All the Main Committees shall, at least three months before the opening of the session, elect a Chairman.

Elections of the other officers provided for in rule 103 shall be held at the latest by the end of the first week of the session.

(b) Each Main Committee, taking into account the closing date for the session fixed by the General Assembly on the recommendation of the General Committee, shall adopt its own priorities and meet as may be necessary to complete the consideration of the items referred to it. It shall at the beginning of the session adopt a programme of work indicating, if possible, a target date for the conclusion of its work, the approximate dates of consideration of items and the number of meetings to be allocated to each item.

Representation of Members

Rule 100

Each Member may be represented by one person on each Main Committee and on any other committee that may be established upon which all Members have the right to be represented. It may also assign to these committees advisers, technical advisers, experts or persons of similar status.

Rule 101

Upon designation by the chairman of the delegation, advisers, technical advisers, experts or persons of similar status may act as members of committees. Persons of this status shall not, however, unless designated as alternate representatives, be eligible for election as Chairmen, Vice-Chairmen or Rapporteurs of committees or for seats in the General Assembly.

Subcommittees

Rule 102

Each committee may set up subcommittees, which shall

elect their own officers.

Election of officers

Rule 103

Each Main Committee shall elect a Chairman, three Vice-Chairmen and a Rapporteur. In the case of other committees, each shall elect a Chairman, one or more Vice-Chairmen and a Rapporteur. These officers shall be elected on the basis of equitable geographical distribution, experience and personal competence. The elections shall be held by secret ballot unless the committee decides otherwise in an election where only one candidate is standing. The nomination of each candidate shall be limited to one speaker, after which the committee shall immediately proceed to the election.

The Chairman of a Main Committee shall not vote

Rule 104

The Chairman of a Main Committee shall not vote, but another member of his delegation may vote in his place.

Absence of officers

Rule 105

If the Chairman finds it necessary to be absent during a meeting or any part thereof, he shall designate one of the Vice-Chairmen to take his place. A Vice-Chairman acting as Chairman shall have the same powers and duties as the Chairman. If any officer of the committee is unable to perform his functions, a new officer shall be elected for the unexpired term.

Functions of the Chairman

Rule 106

The Chairman shall declare the opening and closing

of each meeting of the committee, direct its discussions, ensure observance of these rules, accord the right to speak, put questions and announce decisions. He shall rule on points of order and, subject to these rules, shall have complete control of the proceedings at any meeting and over the maintenance of order thereat. The Chairman may, in the course of the discussion of an item, propose to the committee the limitation of the time to be allowed to speakers, the limitation of the number of times each representative may speak, the closure of the list of speakers or the closure of the debate. He may also propose the suspension or the adjournment of the meeting or the adjournment of the debate on the item under discussion.

Rule 107

The Chairman, in the exercise of his functions, remains under the authority of the committee.

Conduct of Business

Quorum

Rule 108

The Chairman may declare a meeting open and permit the debate to proceed when at least one quarter of the members of the committee are present. The presence of a majority of the members shall be required for any decision to be taken.

Speeches

Rule 109

No representative may address the committee without having previously obtained the permission of the Chairman.

The Chairman shall call upon speakers in the order in which they signify their desire to speak. The Chairman may call a speaker to order if his remarks are not relevant to the subject under discussion.

Congratulations

Rule 110

Congratulations to the officers of a Main Committee shall not be expressed except by the Chairman of the previous session - or, in his absence, by a member of his delegation - after all the officers of the Committee have been elected.

Precedence

Rule 111

The Chairman and the Rapporteur of a committee or subcommittee may be accorded precedence for the purpose of explaining the conclusions arrived at by their committee or subcommittee.

Statements by the Secretariat

Rule 112

The Secretary-General, or a member of the Secretariat designated by him as his representative, may at any time make either oral or written statements to any committee or subcommittee concerning any question under consideration by it.

Points of order

Rule 113

During the discussion of any matter, a representative may rise to a point of order, and the point of order shall be immediately decided by the Chairman in accordance with the rules of procedure. A representative may appeal against the ruling of the Chairman. The appeal shall be immediately put to the vote, and the Chairman's ruling shall stand unless overruled by a majority of the members present and voting. A representative rising to a point of order may not speak on the substance of the matter under discussion.

Time limit on speeches

Rule 114

The committee may limit the time to be allowed to each speaker and the number of times each representative may speak on any question. Before a decision is taken, two representatives may speak in favour of, and two against, a proposal to set such limits. When the debate is limited and a representative exceeds his allotted time, the Chairman shall call him to order without delay.

Closing of list of speakers, right of reply

Rule 115

During the course of a debate, the Chairman may announce the list of speakers and, with the consent of the committee, declare the list closed. He may, however, accord the right of reply to any member if a speech delivered after he has declared the list closed makes this desirable.

Adjournment of debate

Rule 116

During the discussion of any matter, a representative may move the adjournment of the debate on the item under discussion. In addition to the proposer of the motion, two representatives may speak in favour of, and two against, the motion, after which the motion shall be immediately put to the vote. The Chairman may limit the time to be allowed to speakers under this rule.

Closure of debate

Rule 117

A representative may at any time move the closure of the debate on the item under discussion, whether or not any other representative has signified his wish to speak. Permission to speak on the closure of the debate shall be accorded only to two speakers opposing the closure, after which the motion shall be immediately put to the vote. If the committee is in favour of the closure, the Chairman shall declare the closure of the debate. The Chairman may limit the time to be allowed to speakers under this rule.

Suspension or adjournment of the meeting

Rule 118

During the discussion of any matter, a representative may move the suspension or the adjournment of the meeting. Such motions shall not be debated but shall be immediately put to the vote. The Chairman may limit the time to be allowed to the speaker moving the suspension or adjournment of the meeting.

Order of procedural motions

Rule 119

Subject to rule 113, the motions indicated below shall have precedence in the following order over all other proposals or motions before the meeting:

(a) To suspend the meeting;

(b) To adjourn the meeting;

(c) To adjourn the debate on the item under discussion;

(d) To close the debate on the item under discussion.

Proposals and amendments

Rule 120

Proposals and amendments shall normally be submitted in writing to the Secretary-General, who shall circulate copies to the delegations.

As a general rule, no proposal shall be discussed or put to the vote at any meeting of the committee unless copies of it have been circulated to all delegations not later than the day preceding the meeting.

The Chairman may, however, permit the discussion and consideration of amendments, or of motions as to procedure, even though such amendments and motions have not been circulated or have only been circulated the same day.

Decisions on competence

Rule 121

Subject to rule 119, any motion calling for a decision on the competence of the committee to adopt a proposal submitted to it shall be put to the vote before a vote is taken on the proposal in question.

Withdrawal of motions

Rule 122

A motion may be withdrawn by its proposer at any time before voting on it has commenced, provided that the motion has not been amended. A motion thus withdrawn may be reintroduced by any member.

Reconsideration of proposals

Rule 123

When a proposal has been adopted or rejected, it may not be reconsidered at the same session unless the committee, by a two-thirds majority of the members present and voting, so decides.

Permission to speak on a motion to reconsider shall be accorded only to two speakers opposing the motion, after which it shall be immediately put to the vote.

Voting

Voting rights

Rule 124

Each member of the committee shall have one vote.

Majority required

Rule 125

Decisions of committees shall be made by a majority of the members present and voting.

Meaning of the phrase "members present and voting"

Rule 126

For the purposes of these rules, the phrase "members present and voting" means members casting an affirmative or negative vote. Members which abstain from voting are considered as not voting.

Method of voting

Rule 127

(a) The committee shall normally vote by show of hands or by standing, but any representative may request a roll-call. The roll-call shall be taken in the English alphabetical order of the names of the members, beginning with the member whose name is drawn by lot by the Chairman. The name of each member shall be called in any roll-call, and its representative shall reply "yes", "no" or "abstention". The result of the voting shall be inserted in the record in the English alphabetical order of the names of the members.

(b) When the committee votes by mechanical means, a non-recorded vote shall replace a vote by show of hands or by standing and a recorded vote shall replace a roll-call vote. Any representative may request a recorded vote. In the case of a recorded vote, the committee shall, unless a representative requests otherwise, dispense with the procedure of calling out the names of the members; nevertheless, the result of the voting shall be inserted in the record in the same manner as that of a roll-call vote.

Conduct during voting

Rule 128

After the Chairman has announced the beginning of voting, no representative shall interrupt the voting except on a point of order in connection with the actual conduct of the voting. The Chairman may permit members to explain their votes, either before or after the voting, except when the vote is taken by secret ballot. The Chairman may limit the time to be allowed for such explanations. The Chairman shall not permit the proposer of a proposal or of an amendment to explain his vote on his own proposal or amendment.

Division of proposals and amendments

Rule 129

A representative may move that parts of a proposal or of an amendment should be voted on separately. If objection is made to the request for division, the motion for division shall be voted upon. Permission to speak on the motion for division shall be given only to two speakers in favour and two speakers against. If the motion for division is carried, those parts of the proposal or of the amendment which are approved shall then be put to the vote as a whole. If all operative parts of the proposal or of the amendment have been rejected, the proposal or the amendment shall be considered to have been rejected as a whole.

Voting on amendments

Rule 130

When an amendment is moved to a proposal, the amendment shall be voted on first. When two or more amendments are moved to a proposal, the committee shall first vote on the amendment furthest removed in substance from the original proposal and then on the amendment next furthest removed therefrom, and so on until all the amendments have been put to the vote. Where, however, the adoption of one amendment necessarily implies the rejection of another amendment, the latter amendment shall not be put to the vote. If one or more amendments are adopted, the amended proposal shall then be voted upon. A motion is considered an amendment to a proposal if it merely adds to, deletes from or revises part of the proposal.

Voting on proposals

Rule 131

If two or more proposals relate to the same question, the committee shall, unless it decides otherwise, vote on the proposals in the order in which they have been submitted. The committee may, after each vote on a proposal, decide whether to vote on the next proposal.

Elections

Rule 132

When only one person or Member is to be elected and

no candidate obtains in the first ballot the majority required, a second ballot shall be taken, which shall be restricted to the two candidates obtaining the largest number of votes. If in the second ballot the votes are equally divided, and a majority is required, the Chairman shall decide between the candidates by drawing lots.

Equally divided votes

Rule 133

If a vote is equally divided on matters other than elections, the proposal shall be regarded as rejected.

XIV. Admission of New Members to the United Nations

Applications

Rule 134

Any State which desires to become a Member of the United Nations shall submit an application to the Secretary-General. Such application shall contain a declaration, made in a formal instrument, that the State in question accepts the obligations contained in the Charter.

Notification of applications

Rule 135

The Secretary-General shall, for information, send a copy of the application to the General Assembly, or to the Members of the United Nations if the Assembly is not in session.

Consideration of applications and decision thereon

Rule 136

If the Security Council recommends the applicant State

for membership, the General Assembly shall consider whether the applicant is a peace-loving State and is able and willing to carry out the obligations contained in the Charter and shall decide, by a two-thirds majority of the members present and voting, upon its application for membership.

Rule 137

If the Security Council does not recommend the applicant State for membership or postpones the consideration of the application, the General Assembly may, after full consideration of the special report of the Security Council, send the application back to the Council, together with a full record of the discussion in the Assembly, for further consideration and recommendation or report.

Notification of decision and effective date of membership

Rule 138

The Secretary-General shall inform the applicant State of the decision of the General Assembly. If the application is approved, membership shall become effective on the date on which the General Assembly takes its decision on the application.

XV. Elections to Principal Organs

General Provisions

Terms of office

Rule 139

Except as provided in rule 147, the term of office of members of Councils shall begin on 1 January following their election by the General Assembly and shall end on 31 December following the election of their successors.

By-elections

Rule 140

Should a member cease to belong to a Council before its term of office expires, a by-election shall be held separately at the next session of the General Assembly to elect a member for the unexpired term.

Secretary-General

Appointment of the Secretary-General

Rule 141

When the Security Council has submitted its recommendation on the appointment of the Secretary-General, the General Assembly shall consider the recommendation and vote upon it by secret ballot in private meeting.

Security Council

Annual elections

Rule 142

The General Assembly shall each year, in the course of its regular session, elect five non-permanent members of the Security Council for a term of two years [Under paragraph 3 of resolution 1991 A (XVIII) of 17 December 1963, the General Assembly decided that "the ten non-permanent members of the Security Council shall be elected according to the following pattern: "(a) Five from African and Asian States; "(b) One from Eastern European States; "(c) Two from Latin American States; "(d) Two from Western European and other States."].

Qualifications for membership

Rule 143

In the election of non-permanent members of the

Security Council, due regard shall, in accordance with Article 23, paragraph 1, of the Charter, be specially paid, in the first instance, to the contribution of Members of the United Nations to the maintenance of international peace and security and to the other purposes of the Organization, and also to equitable geographical distribution [Under paragraph 3 of resolution 1991 A (XVIII), the General Assembly decided that "the ten non-permanent members of the Security Council shall be elected according to the following pattern: "(a) Five from African and Asian States; "(b) One from Eastern European States; "(c) Two from Latin American States; "(d) Two from Western European and other States."].

Re-eligibility

Rule 144

A retiring member of the Security Council shall not be eligible for immediate re-election.

Economic and Social Council

Annual elections

Rule 145

The General Assembly shall each year, in the course of its regular session, elect eighteen members of the Economic and Social Council for a term of three years [Under paragraph 4 of resolution 2847 (XXVI), the General Assembly decided that "the members of the Economic and Social Council shall be elected according to the following pattern: "(a) Fourteen members from African States; "(b) Eleven members from Asian States; "(c) Ten members from Latin American States; "(d) Thirteen members from Western European and other States; "(e) Six members from socialist States of Eastern Europe."].

Re-eligibility

Rule 146

A retiring member of the Economic and Social Council shall be eligible for immediate re-election.

Trusteeship Council

Occasions for elections

Rule 147

When a Trusteeship Agreement has been approved and a Member of the United Nations has become an Administering Authority of a Trust Territory in accordance with Article 83 or Article 85 of the Charter, the General Assembly shall hold such election or elections to the Trusteeship Council as may be necessary, in accordance with Article 86. A Member or Members elected at any such election at a regular session shall take office immediately upon their election and shall complete their terms in accordance with the provisions of rule 139 as if they had begun their terms of office on 1 January following their election.

Terms of office and re-eligibility

Rule 148

A non-administering member of the Trusteeship Council shall be elected for a term of three years and shall be eligible for immediate re-election.

Vacancies

Rule 149

At each session the General Assembly shall, in accordance with Article 86 of the Charter, elect members to fill any vacancies.

International Court of Justice

Method of election

Rule 150

The election of the members of the International Court of Justice shall take place in accordance with the Statute of the Court.

Rule 151

Any meeting of the General Assembly held in pursuance of the Statute of the International Court of Justice for the purpose of electing members of the Court shall continue until as many candidates as are required for all the seats to be filled have obtained in one or more ballots an absolute majority of votes.

XVI. Administrative and Budgetary Questions

General Provisions

Regulations for financial administration

Rule 152

The General Assembly shall establish regulations for the financial administration of the United Nations [For the Financial Regulations and Rules of the United Nations, see ST/SGB/2003/7].

Financial implications of resolutions

Rule 153

No resolution involving expenditure shall be recommended by a committee for approval by the General Assembly unless it is accompanied by an estimate of expenditures prepared by the Secretary-General. No resolution in respect of which expenditures are anticipated by the Secretary-General shall be voted by the General Assembly until the Administrative and Budgetary Committee (Fifth Committee) has had an opportunity of stating the effect of the proposal upon the budget estimates of the United Nations.

Rule 154

The Secretary-General shall keep all committees informed of the detailed estimated cost of all resolutions which have been recommended by the committees for approval by the General Assembly.

Advisory Committee on Administrative and Budgetary Questions

Appointment

Rule 155

The General Assembly shall appoint an Advisory Committee on Administrative and Budgetary Questions consisting of sixteen members, including at least three financial experts of recognized standing.

Composition

Rule 156

The members of the Advisory Committee on Administrative and Budgetary Questions, no two of whom shall be nationals of the same State shall be selected on the basis of broad geographical representation, personal qualifications and experience and shall serve for a period of three years corresponding to three calendar years. Members shall retire by rotation and shall be eligible for reappointment.

The three financial experts shall not retire simultaneously. The General Assembly shall appoint the members of the Advisory Committee at the regular session immediately preceding the expiration of the term of office of the members or, in case of vacancies, at the next session.

Functions

Rule 157

The Advisory Committee on Administrative and Budgetary Questions shall be responsible for expert examination of the programme budget of the United Nations and shall assist the Administrative and Budgetary Committee (Fifth Committee).

At the beginning of each regular session at which the proposed programme budget for the following biennium is to be considered, it shall submit to the General Assembly a detailed report on the proposed programme budget for that biennium.

It shall also submit, at such times as may be specified in the applicable provisions of the Financial Regulations and Rules of the United Nations [See ST/SGB/2003/7], a report on the accounts of the United Nations and all United Nations entities for which the Secretary-General has administrative responsibility.

It shall examine on behalf of the General Assembly the administrative budgets of specialized agencies and proposals for financial and budgetary arrangements with such agencies. It shall perform such other duties as may be assigned to it under the Financial Regulations of the United Nations.

Committee on Contributions

Appointment

Rule 158

The General Assembly shall appoint an expert Committee on Contributions consisting of eighteen members.

Composition

Rule 159

The members of the Committee on Contributions, no two of whom shall be nationals of the same State, shall be selected on the basis of broad geographical representation, personal qualifications and experience and shall serve for a period of three years corresponding to three calendar years. Members shall retire by rotation and shall be eligible for reappointment. The General Assembly shall appoint the members of the Committee on Contributions at the regular session immediately preceding the expiration of the term of office of the members or, in case of vacancies, at the next session.

Functions

Rule 160

The Committee on Contributions shall advise the General Assembly concerning the apportionment, under Article 17, paragraph 2, of the Charter, of the expenses of the Organization among Members, broadly according to capacity to pay.

The scale of assessments, when once fixed by the General Assembly, shall not be subject to a general revision for at least three years unless it is clear that there have been substantial changes in relative capacity to pay.

The Committee shall also advise the General Assembly on the assessments to be fixed for new Members, on appeals by Members for a change of assessments and on the action to be taken with regard to the application of Article 19 of the Charter.

XVII. Subsidiary Organs of the General Assembly

Establishment and rules of procedure

Rule 161

The General Assembly may establish such subsidiary organs as it deems necessary for the performance of its functions [Sentence reproducing textually a provision of the Charter (Art. 22)]. The rules relating to the procedure of committees of the General Assembly, as well as rules 45 and 60, shall apply to the procedure of any subsidiary organ unless the Assembly or the subsidiary organ decides otherwise.

XVIII. Interpretation and Amendments

Italicized headings

Rule 162

The italicized headings of these rules, which were inserted for reference purposes only, shall be disregarded in the interpretation of the rules.

Method of Amendment

Rule 163

These rules of procedure may be amended by a decision of the General Assembly, taken by a majority of the members present and voting, after a committee has reported on the proposed amendment.

Annexes

Annex I (A)

Recommendations and suggestions of the Special Committee on Methods and Procedures of the General Assembly approved by the Assembly (b)

Consideration by the General Assembly of international conventions negotiated by conferences of government representatives of all Member States

13. The Special Committee found that in the past some of the Main Committees of the General Assembly had devoted a particularly large number of meetings to the detailed consideration, article by article, of texts of international conventions. This was even the case where the text of a convention had been drawn up by an international conference on which all Member States had been represented. It was pointed out in this connection that experience had shown that a Main Committee, by the very fact of its size, was not particularly fitted to draft conventions, and that when it was entrusted with the detailed study of conventions, it often did not have time to deal satisfactorily with the other questions for which it was responsible.

The Special Committee recognizes the importance of the sponsorship of conventions by the General Assembly. It believes that the authority of the General Assembly and the powerful influence its debates have on public opinion should, in many cases, be used for the benefit of international cooperation. It therefore favours the retention by the General Assembly of the necessary freedom of action.

The Special Committee therefore confines itself to recommending that when conventions have been negotiated by international conferences in which all the Members of the United Nations have been invited to take part, and on which they have been represented, not only by experts acting in a personal capacity but by representatives of Governments, and when these conventions are subsequently submitted to the General Assembly for consideration, the Assembly should not undertake a further detailed examination, but should limit itself to discussing them in a broad manner and to giving its general views on the instruments submitted to it.

After such a debate, the General Assembly could, if desirable, adopt the conclusions reached by the conferences and recommend to Members the acceptance or ratification of such conventions.

This procedure might be applied in particular to conventions submitted to the General Assembly as a result of conferences of all Member States convened by the Economic and Social Council under Article 62, paragraph 4, of the Charter.

Consideration by the General Assembly of international conventions prepared by experts or by conferences in which not all Member States take part - drafting of legal texts

14. Furthermore, when it is proposed that the General Assembly should consider conventions prepared by groups of experts not acting as governmental representatives, or by conferences in which not all Members of the United Nations have been invited to take part, it would be advisable for the General Committee and the General Assembly to determine whether one of the Main Committees, especially the Legal Committee, would have enough time during the session to examine these conventions in detail, or whether it would be possible to set up an ad hoc committee to undertake this study during the session.

If this is not possible, the Special Committee recommends that the General Assembly should decide, after or without a general debate on the fundamental principles of the proposed convention, that an ad hoc committee should be established to meet between sessions.

Alternatively, the General Assembly might decide to convene a conference of plenipotentiaries, between two of its own sessions, to study, negotiate, draft, and possibly sign, the convention. The conference of plenipotentiaries might be empowered by the General Assembly to transmit the instruments directly to Governments for acceptance or ratification. In this case too, the General Assembly might, at a subsequent session, express its general opinion on the convention resulting from the conference, and might recommend to Members its acceptance or ratification.

With regard to the drafting of legal texts, the Special Committee strongly recommends that small drafting committees should be resorted to whenever possible.

Meetings of the General Committee and of the Main Committees

20. In order that more frequent meetings of the General Committee should not delay the work of plenary and committee meetings, the Special Committee wishes to mention that it would be desirable for the General Committee to be enabled to meet, whenever necessary, at the same time as the plenary or the Main Committees. (In such cases, one of the Vice-Presidents could take the chair at plenary meetings and the Vice-Chairman could replace the Chairman at Main Committee meetings.)

The Special Committee also considers that, in order to save time at the beginning of the session, some of the Main Committees should not wait until the end of the general debate before starting their work.

Allocation of agenda items to the Main Comittees

22. In the past, some of the Main Committees have been allocated more items requiring prolonged consideration than have others. This has especially been the case for the First Committee. The Special Committee noted, however, that, during the third session of the General Assembly, exception had been made to the principle laid down in rule 89 [Rule 97 of the present rules of procedure], that "items relating to the same category of subjects shall be referred to the committee or committees dealing with that category of subjects".

The Special Committee feels that the allocation of items to committees might be effected in a less rigid manner and that questions which may be considered as falling within the competence of two or more committees should preferably be referred to the committee with the lightest agenda.

Consideration of agenda items in plenary meetings without prior reference to a Main Committee

23. Another means of lightening the task of any given Main Committee would be to consider directly in plenary meeting, without preliminary reference to committee, certain questions which fall within the terms of reference of the Main Committee. This procedure would, moreover, have the great advantage of reducing to a notable extent repetition of debate.

It is felt that the amount of time saved by this method would be considerable, especially if the Main Committee and plenary meetings could be held concurrently.

If the Main Committee could not meet at the same time as the plenary meeting, the fact that the Committee was not meeting would enable another Main Committee to meet in its place.

The consideration of questions in plenary meetings would have the benefit of the attendance of leaders of delegations and of greater solemnity and publicity. The slightly higher cost to the United Nations of plenary meetings, due in particular to the distribution of verbatim records of the meetings, would undoubtedly be compensated by the shorter duration of the session.

The General Committee would be responsible for suggesting to the General Assembly which items on the agenda might be dealt with in this manner. The Special Committee recommends that this method should be introduced on an experimental basis at future sessions.

The Special Committee is of the opinion that this procedure would be especially appropriate for certain questions the essential aspects of which are already familiar to Members, such as items which have been considered by the General Assembly at previous sessions and which do not require either the presence of representatives of non-member States or the hearing of testimony.

The role of the President of the General Assembly, of the Chairmen of committees and of the Secretariat

39. At this point the Special Committee desires to stress once more the importance of the role of the President of the General Assembly and of the Chairmen of committees. The satisfactory progress of the proceedings depends essentially on their competence, authority, tact and impartiality, their respect for the rights both of minorities as well as majorities, and their familiarity with the rules of procedure. The General Assembly, or the committee, as the case may be, is the master of the conduct of its own proceedings. It is, however, the

special task of the Chairmen to guide the proceedings of these bodies in the best interests of all the Members.

The Special Committee considers that everything possible should be done to help Chairmen in the discharge of these important functions. The President of the General Assembly and the General Committee should assist the Chairmen of committees with their advice. The Secretary-General should place his experience and all his authority at their disposal.

The Special Committee is happy to note the Secretariat's valuable practice of holding daily meetings of the committee secretaries, under the chairmanship of the Executive Assistant to the Secretary-General, where the procedural questions arising from day to day in the General Assembly and committees are thoroughly examined. Furthermore, the Special Committee stresses the value of having, as in the past, a legal adviser from the Secretariat in attendance at meetings to give the Chairmen or the committees such advice as they need for the conduct of their business and the interpretation of the rules of procedure.

Annex II (A)

Methods and procedures of the General Assembly for dealing with legal and drafting questions (b)

Part 1

Recommendations of the General Assembly

The General Assembly, ...

1. Recommends:

(a) That, whenever any Committee contemplates making a recommendation to the General Assembly to request an advisory opinion from the International Court of Justice, the matter may, at some appropriate stage of its consideration by that Committee, be referred to the Sixth Committee for advice on the legal aspects and on the drafting of the request, or the Committee concerned may propose that the matter should be considered by a joint Committee of itself and the Sixth Committee;

(b) That, whenever any Committee contemplates making a recommendation to the General Assembly to refer a matter to the International Law Commission, the Committee may, at some appropriate stage of its consideration, consult the Sixth Committee as to the advisability of such a reference and on its drafting;

(c) That, whenever any Committee contemplates making a recommendation for the adoption by the General Assembly of any amendment to the rules of procedure of the General Assembly, the matter shall, at some appropriate stage of its consideration by that Committee, be referred to the Sixth Committee for advice on the drafting of such amendment and of any consequential amendment;

(d) That, when a Committee considers the legal aspects of a question important, the Committee should refer it for legal advice to the Sixth Committee or propose that the question should be considered by a joint Committee of itself and the Sixth Committee.

Part 2

Excerpts from the report of the Special Committee for the Consideration of the Methods and Procedures of the

General Assembly for Dealing with Legal and Drafting Questions

Allocation of agenda items to the Main Committees

19. As to the first of those problems [namely, the allocation of agenda items to the Main Committees by the General Assembly at the outset of each session], the Special Committee recalled that rule 97 of the rules of procedure of the General Assembly provided that "Items relating to the same category of subjects shall be referred to the committee or committees dealing with that category of subjects ..." It also noted that a recommendation of the Special Committee on Methods and Procedures, approved by the General Assembly in resolution 362 (IV) of 22 October 1949 and annexed to the rules of procedure, provided that "... questions which may be considered as falling within the competence of two or more committees should preferably be referred to the committee with the lightest agenda".

20. In view of those provisions, the present Special Committee did not find it necessary to make any formal recommendation on the allocation of agenda items at the opening of each session. It was confident that the General Committee, in making recommendations to the General Assembly on the distribution of agenda items, would continue to bear in mind the Sixth Committee's function, laid down in rule 99 [Rule 98 of the present rules of procedure] of the rules of procedure, as the Legal Committee.

Drafting of complex legal instruments

29. During the course of the discussion [on the question of the drafting of complex legal instruments such as international agreements, statutes of tribunals, etc.] it was pointed out

that the Special Committee on Methods and Procedures, in paragraphs 13 and 14 of its report, approved by General Assembly resolution 362 (IV) of 22 October 1949 and annexed to the rules of procedure [See annex I], made certain recommendations concerning the drafting of conventions, and concluded: "With regard to the drafting of legal texts, the Special Committee strongly recommends that small drafting committees should be resorted to whenever possible."

30. The Special Committee was in complete agreement with those recommendations and, in view of their previous approval by the General Assembly, did not find it necessary to adopt a new provision on the subject. However, the Special Committee considered it desirable that that point should be reaffirmed in its report. On that understanding, the United Kingdom withdrew its draft proposal. [This proposal (A/AC.604/L.18) provided: "That, in principle, the drafting of all clauses, texts or instruments of the following kinds should be either carried out, or, at some appropriate stage, reviewed, by a body of experts legally qualified to do so: "(a) Any regulation for adoption by the General Assembly;

"(b) The terms of reference, functions and powers of subsidiary organs or tribunals hereafter set up by the General Assembly; "(c) Any convention, declaration, agreement or other similar international instrument drawn up under the auspices of the General Assembly, and the drafting of which is to be effected by the Assembly itself, including agreements or instruments to which the United Nations as an Organization is to be a party."]

Drafting of General Assembly resolutions

35. In addition to the above proposals [Proposal by El

Salvador (A/AC.60/L.20) which was withdrawn in favour of a revised text (A/AC.60/L.20/Rev.1) incorporating amendments by the United Kingdom (A/AC.60/L.21), Belgium and Egypt. This revised text, which was worded as follows, was included in the recommendations of the Special Committee to the General Assembly: "(e) That, normally, the Chairman of a Committee shall, at the appropriate time, call upon the Vice-Chairman and the Rapporteur to join him for the purpose of proceeding, in consultation with the competent officials of the Secretariat, to examine the draft resolutions from the point of view of style, form and the use of technical terms, and, when appropriate, to suggest to the Committee such changes as they deem necessary."], the United Kingdom submitted a draft (A/AC.60/L.22) which provided for periodic meetings of the rapporteurs of Committees with the competent officials of the Secretariat to establish, insofar as practicable, common methods of drafting and to ensure that in general the drafting of resolutions was satisfactory from the point of view of style, form and the use of technical terms.

36. It was pointed out that there might be certain practical difficulties in arranging for periodic meetings of rapporteurs. The Special Committee decided to make no formal recommendation on the subject, nevertheless, the Committee believes that it is desirable that informal consultation should take place from time to time between the various rapporteurs and officials of the Secretariat for the purpose described in the United Kingdom proposal.

Reports of the Secretary-General under General Assembly resolution 362 (IV)

37. The United Kingdom submitted a draft proposal (A/AC.60/L.23) suggesting that the Secretary-General should

be requested to furnish to the General Assembly an annual report on the matters dealt with by the Special Committee, indicating to what extent the Assembly or its Committees had succeeded during the year in realizing the objectives aimed at and suggesting any appropriate adjustments or improvements in the methods and procedures involved.

38. During the discussion, the representative of the Secretary-General recalled that the General Assembly, in paragraph 6 of resolution 362 (IV) of 22 October 1949, had requested the Secretary-General "to carry out appropriate studies and to submit, at such times as he may consider appropriate, suitable proposals for the improvement of the methods and procedures of the General Assembly and its committees ...". It was pointed out that the Secretary-General was much concerned with improving the procedures and methods of the Assembly and that there was no need for a new resolution requesting reports on that subject.

39. The Special Committee agreed that the points covered by the United Kingdom draft could be included when advisable in reports of the Secretary-General under resolution 362 (IV); such reports should be submitted at the appropriate times, and at reasonably frequent intervals. Consequently, the United Kingdom draft was withdrawn, and the Committee made no formal recommendation on the subject.

Annex III

Resolution 1898 (XVIII) adopted on the recommendation of the Ad Hoc Committee on the Improvement of the Methods of Work of the General Assembly (a)

The General Assembly,

Recalling with appreciation the initiative taken by the President of the sixteenth session of the General Assembly in his memorandum of 26 April 1962 on the methods of work of the Assembly, [Official Records of the General Assembly, Seventeenth Session, Annexes, agenda item 86, document A/5123].

Recalling its decision of 30 October 1962 establishing the Ad Hoc Committee on the Improvement of the Methods of Work of the General Assembly and its resolution 1845 (XVII) of 19 December 1962, by which it decided to continue the Committee,

Having considered the report submitted by the Ad Hoc Committee in pursuance of the above-mentioned resolution, [Official Records of the General Assembly, Eighteenth Session, Annexes, agenda item 25, document A/5423]

Conscious of the need to adapt its methods of work to the changed circumstances in the General Assembly, in particular those resulting from the recent increase in the number of Member States,

Concerned however to avoid reducing in any way the possibilities for action available to the General Assembly under the Charter of the United Nations and the rules of procedure of the Assembly,

Convinced that it is in the interests of the Organization and of Member States that the work of the General Assembly should be carried out as efficiently and expeditiously as possible and that, save in quite exceptional cases, the duration of regular sessions should not exceed thirteen weeks,

Takes note of the observations contained in the report

of the Ad Hoc Committee on the Improvement of the Methods of Work of the General Assembly and approves the recommendations submitted by the Committee, in particular those which provide that:

(a) The President of the General Assembly should make every effort to ensure that the general debate proceeds in a methodical and regular manner, and should close the list of speakers, with the consent of the Assembly, as soon as he considers it feasible;

(b) All the Main Committees, except the First Committee, should begin their work not later than two working days after they have received the list of agenda items referred to them by the General Assembly;

(c) The First Committee should meet as soon as possible to organize its work, determine the order of discussion of the items allocated to it and start the systematic consideration of its agenda; at the beginning of the session, such meetings might be held when there is an interruption in the general debate; later, plenary meetings might be held during one part of the day, the other part being reserved for the First Committee, thus enabling the Committee to proceed with its regular work as soon as possible after the opening of the session;

(d) Each of the Main Committees should establish its programme of work as soon as possible, including the approximate dates on which it will consider the various items referred to it and the date on which it proposes to conclude its work, on the understanding that this programme will be transmitted to the General Committee to enable it to make such recommendations as it may deem relevant, including, when the General

Committee considers it appropriate, recommendations as to the dates by which Main Committees should conclude their work;

(e) Each of the Main Committees should consider the establishment, in the circumstances referred to in paragraphs 29 to 32 of the report of the Ad Hoc Committee, [These paragraphs read as follows: "29. The increase in the number of Members of the United Nations has created a situation in which it frequently happens that more than 100 delegations are present and most of them participate in the debates in the Main Committees. Although the presence of such a large number of delegations involves no practical difficulties when statements of the positions of Governments are being made, it makes it more difficult to discuss concrete points, to have a rapid exchange of views on subjects where ideas differ or to draft and modify texts. The Committee is of the opinion that in many cases the examination of agenda items by the committees would be greatly facilitated if, as soon as possible and especially when the main points of view have been expressed, the committee decided, on the initiative of its Chairman or of one or more of its members, to set up a subcommittee or working group, in conformity with rule 104 [now 102] of the rules of procedure (98 [now 96] in the case of the plenary Assembly). This procedure might be particularly helpful when there is general agreement on the question under discussion but disagreement on points of detail. "30. The Ad Hoc Committee would recall in this connection that in the course of the first sessions of the General Assembly frequent use was made of subcommittees and working groups and that they were of great assistance to the General Assembly in the preparation of texts which to this day govern the structures of the United Nations in the formulation of important international instruments and in the solution of difficult political problems (one example is the sub-committee which dealt with the future status of the former Italian colonies). As far back as 1947, the report of the Committee on Procedures and Organization expressed itself on this subject as follows: "'The Main Committees should consider carefully at an early stage in their work how their programmes might be expedited by the establishment of sub-committees. It is, of course, impossible to adopt fixed rules on this matter. If the debate in full committee showed that there was general agreement on the question under discussion but disagreement on points of detail, it would clearly be desirable to set up a small drafting committee to prepare a resolution for submission to the Main Committee. Technical questions on which there is no substantial disagreement should be referred to sub-committees as quickly as possible. In some cases the work of sub-committees would be facilitated by working informally, and on occasion, in private.' (A/388, para. 21.) "31. The subcommittees or working groups could, in most cases, consist of representatives of the delegations with the closest interest in the agenda item, representatives who are especially competent to deal with the problem under discussion and others chosen in such a way as to ensure that the sub-committee or working group will be broadly representative, geographically and politically. "32. These bodies could meet either in public or in private, according to the circumstances, and could either follow formal procedures or discuss matters informally. Their function would be to make it possible for those primarily interested in an item to exchange views, thus facilitating subsequent agreement and compromise solutions; they could prepare draft resolutions or at least formulate alternative solutions: they could appoint rapporteurs to present their conclusions and to give the necessary explanations to the committee which established them. The committee itself would be entirely free to take final decisions but, since all aspects of the problem would have been given minute examination, it would undoubtedly find its own work greatly facilitated both with regard to substance and to the time thus saved. It would also often be possible for the committee to consider other items on its agenda while the subcommittee or working group was carrying out its assignment."] of subcommittees or working groups of limited size but representative of its membership, for the purpose of facilitating its work;

(f) The General Committee should fulfil its functions under rules 40, 41 and 42 of the rules of procedure and, in particular, make appropriate recommendations for furthering the progress of the Assembly and its Committees, in such a way as to facilitate the closing of the session by the date fixed; to this end, the General Committee should meet at least once every three weeks;

(g) Presiding officers should make use of the resources provided by the rules of procedure and exercise their prerogatives under rules 35 and 108 [Rule 106 of the present rules of procedure], in order to accelerate the work of the General Assembly; to that effect they should, inter alia:.

(i) Open meetings at the scheduled time;

(ii) Urge representatives to take the floor in the order in which they were inscribed on the list of speakers, it being understood that representatives prevented from so doing will normally be placed at the end of the list, unless they have arranged to change places with other representatives;

(iii) Apply the rules of procedure in such a way as to ensure the proper exercise of the right of reply, explanation of votes and points of order.

Annex IV (A)

Conclusions of the Special Committee on the Rationalization of the Procedures and Organization of the General Assembly

I. Mandate of the Special Committee

1. The members of the Special Committee agreed that the existing rules of procedure were generally satisfactory and that most improvements would be achieved not through changes in the rules of procedure but through better application of the existing rules, due account being taken of the conclusions of the Special Committee and of the various committees responsible for reviewing the procedures and organization of the General Assembly [para. 12 of the report of the Special Committee, Official Records of the General Assembly, Twenty-sixth Session, Supplement No. 26 (A/8426)].

2. The Special Committee considered, moreover, that it would be desirable to review from time to time the procedures and organization of the General Assembly [para. 13].

II. General Organization of Sessions

A. Opening date

3. The Special Committee is of the opinion that it would not be desirable to change the date fixed for the opening of sessions [para. 18].

B. Duration of sessions

4. The Special Committee, noting that, despite the appreciable increase in the number of Member States, it has been possible to maintain an average duration of thirteen weeks for regular sessions, is of the view that this period should not be changed and that, in any case, the session should end before Christmas [para. 22].

5. The Special Committee did not endorse the suggestion that the session should be divided into two parts. The Committee likewise did not endorse the suggestion that the session should theoretically last a whole year and should merely be adjourned after a two-month main session [para. 23].

C. Residuary sessions

6. The Special Committee did not endorse the suggestion that a brief meeting of the General Assembly, to be called a "residuary session", might be held at head-of-mission level about the end of April for the discussion of certain administrative and routine questions [para. 24].

III. General Committee

A. Composition of the General Committee

1. Increase in membership

7. The Special Committee decided not to take any action on the question of either maintaining or increasing the present membership of the General Committee [para. 31].

8. Furthermore, the Special Committee did not retain the suggestion that the Chairman of the Credentials Committee should be authorized to participate in the work of the General Committee [para.32].

2. Absence of members of the General Committee elected in their personal capacity

9. The Special Committee considers that the problems which arise when the Chairman or Vice-Chairman of a Main Committee cannot attend a meeting of the General Committee would be settled for the most part if the General Assembly decided to increase the number of Vice-Chairmen of the Main Committees [para. 36].

10. The Special Committee also considers that, if the General Assembly took such a decision, the Chairman of a Main Committee, in designating a Vice-Chairman as his substitute, should take into account the representative character of the General Committee [para. 37].

B. Functions of the General Committee

1. Importance of the role of the General Committee

11. The Special Committee considers that the General Committee, in view of the functions conferred on it by the rules of procedure, should play a major role in advancing the rational organization and general conduct of the proceedings of the General Assembly. The Committee is of the opinion that the General Committee should discharge completely and effectively the functions assigned to it under rules 40, 41 and 42 of the rules of procedure, the purpose of which is to assist the Assembly in the general conduct of its work [para. 41].

2. Adoption of the agenda and allocation of items

12. The Special Committee recommends that, within the framework of the functions conferred on it by the rules of procedure, and subject to the limitation prescribed in rule 40 as regards the discussion of the substance of an item, the General Committee should examine the provisional agenda, together with the supplementary list and requests for the inclusion of additional items, more attentively and carry out more fully and consistently its functions of recommending with regard to each item its inclusion in the agenda, the rejection of the request for inclusion or its inclusion in the provisional agenda of a future session, as well as of allocating items to the Main Committees, regard being had to rules 99 and 101[Rules 97 and 98 of the present rules of procedure] of the rules of procedure, with a view to ensuring that all items inscribed on the agenda can be taken up by the end of the session [para.45].

3. Organization of the work of the General Assembly

13. The Special Committee recalls the recommendation, in subparagraph (f) of General Assembly resolution 1898 (XVIII) [See annex III], that the General Committee should meet at least once every three weeks. The Special Committee notes that the recommendation has not been complied with and expresses the hope that the General Committee will be able to hold more frequent meetings, in conformity with rule 42 of the rules of procedure, without thereby interfering with the normal meeting schedule of the plenary and the Main Committees [para. 49].

14. The Special Committee also considers that, in the discharge of the functions conferred by rules 41 and 42 of

the rules of procedure and subject to the limitation prescribed in rule 41 regarding the decision of any political question, the General Committee should review the progress of the General Assembly and the Main Committees and should, as required, assist and make recommendations to the President and the Assembly for the coordination of the proceedings of the Main Committees and for expediting the general conduct of business [para. 50].

C. Ways of facilitating the work of the General Committee

1. Preparatory meetings

15. The Special Committee does not consider that it is in a position to make any recommendation with regard to the holding of preparatory meetings of the General Committee [para. 54].

2. Subsidiary organs

16. The Special Committee does not consider that it is in a position to make any recommendation with regard to the establishment of subsidiary organs of the General Committee [para. 58].

IV. Agenda

A. Presentation and preliminary consideration of the provisional agenda

17. The Special Committee, aware of the need to assist delegations, to the greatest extent possible, to prepare for the work of the General Assembly, recommends to the Assembly that the Secretary-General should be requested:

(a) To communicate to Member States, not later than 15 February, the unofficial list of items proposed for inclusion in the provisional agenda of the Assembly;

(b) To communicate to Member States, not later than 15 June, an annotated list of items which would indicate briefly the history of each item, the available documentation, the substance of the matter to be discussed and earlier decisions by United Nations organs;

(c) To communicate to Member States before the opening of the session an addendum to the annotated list [para. 64].

18. Furthermore, the Special Committee recommends that Member States requesting the inclusion of an item should, if they deem it advisable, make a suggestion concerning its referral to a Main Committee or to the plenary Assembly [para. 65].

B. Reduction in the number of agenda items

1. Non-inclusion of certain items

19. The Special Committee, considering that the General Assembly should take into account the relative importance of agenda items in the light of the purposes and principles of the Charter of the United Nations, recommends to the Assembly that, in the context of rules 22 and 40 of the rules of procedure, Member States should take special interest in the contents of the Assembly's agenda and, in particular, in deciding on the appropriate solution of questions or on the elimination of items which have lost their urgency or relevance, are not ripe for consideration or could be dealt with and even disposed of equally well by subsidiary organs of the General Assembly [para. 70].

2. Staggering of items over two or more years and grouping of related items

20. The Special Committee considers that the staggering

of items over two or more years constitutes one means of rationalizing the procedures of the General Assembly [para. 74].

21. Moreover, the Special Committee recommends to the General Assembly that, as far as possible and appropriate, related items should be grouped under the same title [para. 75].

3. Referral to other organs

22. The Special Committee recommends that the General Assembly should, where relevant, refer specific items to other United Nations organs or to specialized agencies, taking into account the nature of the question [para. 79].

23. The Special Committee also recommends that the General Assembly should give due weight to the debates that have taken place in other organs [para. 80].

4. Non-receivability of certain additional items

24. The Special Committee recommends to the General Assembly that additional items, which are proposed for inclusion in the agenda less than thirty days before the opening of a session, should be included only if the conditions prescribed by rule 15 of the rules of procedure are fully satisfied [para. 84].

C. Allocation of agenda items

1. Division of work among the Main Committees

25. The Special Committee wishes to draw attention to the importance of a rational distribution of agenda items among the Main Committees. In this connection, the Committee, recognizing that the structure of the Main Committees gives them specialization and experience,

recommends that the allocation of agenda items should be based not only on the workload of the Committees but also on the nature of the item, regard being had to rules 99 and 101c of the rules of procedure [para. 89].

26. The Special Committee also considers that it would be helpful if suggestions concerning the allocation of items were made much earlier so that Member States might have more time to study them [para. 90].

27. Lastly, the Special Committee recommends that the General Committee and the General Assembly should consider, in some cases, the possibility of referring more items directly to the plenary [para. 91].

2. Non-referral of certain items to two or more Committees

28. The Special Committee recommends to the General Assembly that agenda items should be so allocated as to ensure, as far as possible, that the same questions or the same aspects of a question are not considered by more than one Committee [para. 95].

V. Organization of the Work of the Main Committees

A. Functions of the individual Committees

29. There was general agreement among the members of the Special Committee that a flexible approach should be adopted towards the whole question of the division of work among the Main Committees and that the Committee should not make any recommendation concerning the referral of specific items, in order not to go beyond its field of competence [para.97].

30. The Special Committee, considering that the potential of the seven Main Committees should be utilized to the full, recommends that the General Assembly should

ensure a more balanced division of work among the Committees, giving due account to the nature of items. The Committee does not, however, feel that it should specify which items might be transferred from one Committee to another [para. 98].

31. The Special Committee, recognizing that the workload of a number of Committees is extremely heavy, is of the opinion that the General Assembly should advise those Committees so to organize their work as to enable them to consider their agenda in the most effective way [para. 99].

1. First Committee

32. The Special Committee, recognizing that the role of the First Committee is essentially political, recommends that this Committee devote itself primarily to problems of peace, security and disarmament [para. 103].

33. The Special Committee, not wishing to make any specific recommendation concerning the allocation of agenda items, did not feel that it should take any decision on the proposal that the reports of the International Atomic Energy Agency and the United Nations Scientific Committee on the Effects of Atomic Radiation should be submitted to the First Committee [para.104].

2. Special Political Committee

34. The Special Committee, reaffirming the major role which must be played by the Special Political Committee and recognizing further that the agenda of that Committee is relatively light, recommends that the General Assembly should consider transferring to the Special Political Committee one or two items usually considered by other Committees

with a view to ensuring a better division of work among the Main Committees [para. 108].

35. The Special Committee did not endorse the suggestions concerning the renaming of the Special Political Committee [para. 109].

3. Second Committee

36. The Special Committee did not feel that it should take any decision on the proposals that all the social aspects of development should be dealt with by the Second Committee. Accordingly, it did not endorse the suggestion to change the name of that Committee [para.113].

4. Third Committee

37. The Special Committee did not feel it should take a decision on the proposal that some of the items on the agenda of the Third Committee should be transferred to other Main Committees [para. 117].

5. Conflicts of competence among Committees

38. The Special Committee considers that conflicts of competence among the Main Committees should be avoided whenever possible. Without prejudging the decision to be taken in each individual case, the Committee wishes to draw attention to the existence of this problem and to the advisability for the General Committee and the General Assembly to consider the most effective ways of remedying it [para. 119].

B. Role of the presiding officers

39. The Special Committee recommends to the General Assembly that the Chairmen of the Main Committees should fully exercise the functions assigned to them in the rules of

procedure and, in particular, make use of the prerogatives given them in rule 108 [Rule 106 of the present rules of procedure] [para. 123].

40. The Special Committee also reaffirms that the Chairmen of the Main Committees should be elected on the basis of equitable geographical distribution as well as on that of experience and competence, as provided for in rule 105 [Rule 103 of the present rules of procedure] of the rules of procedure [para.124].

41. The Special Committee did not endorse the suggestion that candidates should have had at least one year's experience in one of the Main Committees or the suggestion that Chairmen should be elected at the end of the previous session [para. 125]

C. Number of Vice-Chairmen

42. From its own experience, the Special Committee recommends to the General Assembly that its subsidiary organs should consider, as far as possible, the designation of three Vice-Chairmen in order to ensure the representative character of their officers [para. 131].

D. Reports of the Committees

43. The Special Committee, recalling General Assembly resolution 2292 (XXII), recommends to the Assembly that the reports of the Main Committees should be as concise as possible and, save in exceptional cases, should not contain a summary of the debates [para. 133]. [For the recommendations concerning the reports of subsidiary organs, see para. 107 below]

VI. Maximum Utilization of Available Time

A. Plenary Assembly

1. General debate

(a) Frequency

44. The Special Committee, recognizing the unquestionable value of the general debate, considers that it should continue to be held every year and that the time devoted to it should be utilized to the maximum. It wishes to stress also the importance of participation by Heads of State or Government, Ministers for Foreign Affairs and other high officials as a means of enhancing the significance of the general debate [para. 137].

(b) Organization of meetings

(i) Length of the general debate

45. The Special Committee feels that the general debate would be more meaningful, as far as organization was concerned, if it took place intensively and without interruption. Its length should not normally exceed two and a half weeks if the time available were utilized to the maximum [para. 142].

(ii) Closure of the list of speakers

46. Considering that the organization of the general debate would be improved if delegations were required to decide more quickly when to speak, the Special Committee recommends to the General Assembly that the list of speakers wishing to take part in the general debate should be closed at the end of the third day after the opening of the debate [para.144].

(c) Length of statements

47. The Special Committee, noting that during the session commemorating the twenty-fifth anniversary of the

United Nations it had been possible to hear a large number of speakers during a relatively short period without limiting the duration of statements, considers that this result was due to a better utilization of the time available and not to the imposition of a limitation on the length of speeches [para. 147].

48. The Committee notes that during recent sessions of the General Assembly the average length of speeches has been thirty-five minutes and expresses the hope that delegations will ensure that their statements will not be excessively long [para. 148].

(d) Submission of written statements

49. The Special Committee considers that the submission of written statements should not be formally instituted with regard to the general debate [para. 152].

2. Debate on items already considered in Committee

50. The Special Committee is of the opinion that rule 68 [Rule 66 of the present rules of procedure] of the rules of procedure has been applied judiciously and with satisfactory results [para.155].

3. Non-utilization of the rostrum

51. The Special Committee thinks that it would be useful to draw the attention of representatives to the possibility of speaking without going to the rostrum. It considers, however, that in all cases it is for representatives to decide whether they prefer to speak from their seats or from the rostrum, whether on a point of order, for an explanation of vote or in exercise of their right of reply [para.157].

4. Presentation of the reports of the Main Committees

52. The Special Committee wishes to recall the recommendation made in 1947 by the Committee on Procedures and Organization of the General Assembly that Rapporteurs should not read out their reports in plenary meetings [Official Records of the General Assembly, Second Session, Plenary Meetings, vol. II, annex IV, document A/388, para. 26]. It wishes to stress that the presentation of reports in plenary meetings should be limited to brief introductory statements [para. 158].

53. The Special Committee recommends also that the General Assembly should confirm the practice whereby certain related reports of a non-controversial nature may be introduced simultaneously to the plenary Assembly by the Rapporteur [para. 159].

B. Main Committees

1. Nomination of officers

54. The members of the Special Committee agreed that the nomination of candidates involved a significant loss of time. They also recognized that the terms of rule 105 of the rules of procedure, which provided that elections should be held by secret ballot, no longer corresponded to the present practice, since in most cases, as a result of prior consultations, there was only one candidate for each post and voting by secret ballot was therefore superfluous [para. 161]. [Rule 105 (now rule 103) was subsequently amended (see introduction, para. 30 (e))]

55. The Special Committee, bearing in mind particularly the financial implications of such a procedure, did not retain

the suggestion that nominations should be made in writing [para. 162].

56. Furthermore, in view of the dictates of courtesy and the possibility that cases might arise in which nominees would not be known until the last moment, the Special Committee did not deem it advisable to dispense completely with the oral nomination of candidates [para. 163].

57. The Special Committee considers that the nomination of candidates should be limited to one statement for each candidate, after which the Committee would proceed to the election immediately. The Special Committee considers, however, that the general principle that elections are held by secret ballot should be retained [para. 164].

2. Commencement of work

58. The Special Committee recommends that all the Main Committees, with the possible exception of the First Committee, should begin their work on the working day following the receipt of the list of items referred to them by the General Assembly [para. 170].

59. The Special Committee also recommends that the First Committee should be ready to meet whenever no plenary meeting of the Assembly is being held [para. 171].

3. Progress of work

60. The Special Committee recommends that the Main Committees should from time to time review the progress of their work [para. 176].

4. General debate in Committee

61. The Special Committee, while recognizing the unquestionable usefulness and importance of the general

debate, considers that Chairmen should encourage the Main Committees:

(a) To recognize the advisability of shortening the general debate, whenever that is possible without detriment to the work of the Committees;

(b) To extend, whenever appropriate, the practice of holding a single debate on related and logically linked agenda items [para. 180].

62. The Special Committee recognizes that a general debate on questions previously considered by a United Nations organ and covered by a report of the organ concerned should be retained.

The Committee, however, draws the attention of the Chairmen of the Main Committees to the possibility of consulting their Committees in every case when a general debate on a certain item does not seem to be needed.

The Chairmen may resort to this practice to ascertain in particular whether the Committees desire to hold a general debate on every question referred to them by other organs [para. 181].

63. At the same time, the Special Committee wishes to reaffirm that the general debate serves a necessary and very useful purpose in the work of the Main Committees and that its organization should in no circumstances be changed without the consent of the Committees concerned, which therefore should decide on the applicability of the above-mentioned suggestions [para. 182].

64. The Special Committee did not deem it appropriate to make a recommendation concerning the suggestion that delegations sharing the same point of view could use a spokesman who would express those views in a single

statement. Nor did the Committee retain the suggestion that the consideration of certain items already debated in previous sessions might be introduced by specially appointed rapporteurs who would summarize the main issues emerging from previous debates [para. 183].

5. Concurrent consideration of several agenda items

65. The Special Committee considers that in certain cases, when a Main Committee cannot proceed with its discussion of one item, it should be prepared to begin considering the next item on its agenda [para. 187].

6. Establishment of subcommittees or working groups

66. The Special Committee wishes to remind the General Assembly of the desirability of the Main Committees' making use of subcommittees or working groups [para. 188].

C. Measures applicable both to the plenary Assembly and to the Main Committees

1. Opening of meetings at the scheduled time

67. The members of the Special Committee agreed that the General Assembly would operate much more efficiently if the presiding officers made a special effort to open meetings at the scheduled time [para. 190].

68. The Special Committee did not endorse the suggestion to have meetings begin at 9.30 a.m. and 2.30 p.m. in view of the practical difficulties that such a measure would entail [para. 192].

2. List of speakers

69. The Special Committee recommends to the General Assembly that the President of the Assembly or the Chairman of a Main Committee should, soon after the beginning of the

debate on an item, indicate a date for the closing of the list of speakers. He should endeavour to have the list of speakers closed at the latest after one third of the meetings allocated to the item have been held [para. 202].

70. Moreover, the Special Committee considers that speakers should, as far as possible, avoid putting down their names to speak on a given item and at the same time indicating an alternative meeting if they are unable to keep to their original schedule [para. 203].

71. Finally, the Special Committee wishes to reaffirm the practice whereby presiding officers should invite representatives to speak in the order of their inscription on the list of speakers, on the understanding that those prevented from doing so should normally be moved to the end of the list, unless they have arranged to change places with other representatives [para. 204].

3. Limiting the length of speeches or number of speakers

72. The Committee wishes to stress that the amendment on this subject [See introduction, para. 30 (c)] is of a purely technical nature, its only purpose being to limit the number of representatives who could speak on a proposal submitted under rules 74 and 115 [Rules 72 and 114 of the present rules of procedure] of the rules of procedure [para. 210].

73. With regard to the general question of setting a time limit on interventions, the Special Committee, while recognizing that, insofar as possible, statements should be kept brief so as to allow all delegations to present the views of their Governments, considers that no rigid rule on the question could be applied [para. 211].

4. Explanations of vote

74. The Special Committee considers that, in explaining their votes, delegations should limit their statements to an explanation, as brief as possible, of their own votes and should not use the occasion to reopen the debate [para. 216].

75. The Special Committee also considers that presiding officers should be encouraged to use, whenever they deem it appropriate, their powers under rules 90 and 129 [Rules 88 and 128 of the present rules of procedure] of the rules of procedure [para. 217].

76. Finally, the Special Committee recommends to the General Assembly that a delegation should explain its vote only once on the same proposal, in either a Main Committee or a plenary meeting, unless the delegation considers it essential to explain it in both meetings. It recommends further that the sponsor of a draft resolution adopted by a Main Committee should refrain from explaining its vote during the consideration of that draft resolution in the plenary unless it deems it essential to do so [para. 218].

5. Right of reply

77. The Special Committee recommends to the General Assembly that delegations should use restraint in the exercise of their right of reply, both in plenary meetings and in the Main Committees, and that their statements in exercise of that right should be as brief as possible [para. 223].

78. The Special Committee recommends, furthermore, that statements made in the exercise of the right of reply should be delivered, as a general rule, at the end of meetings [para. 224].

6. Points of order

79. The Special Committee recommends to the General Assembly the adoption of the following text as a description of the concept of a point of order [para. 229]:

"(a) A point of order is basically an intervention directed to the presiding officer, requesting him to make use of some power inherent in his office or specifically given him under the rules of procedure. It may, for example, relate to the manner in which the debate is conducted, to the maintenance of order, to the observance of the rules of procedure or to the way in which presiding officers exercise the powers conferred upon them by the rules. Under a point of order, a representative may request the presiding officer to apply a certain rule of procedure or he may question the way in which the officer applies the rule. Thus, within the scope of the rules of procedure, representatives are enabled to direct the attention of the presiding officer to violations or misapplications of the rules by other representatives or by the presiding officer himself. A point of order has precedence over any other matter, including procedural motions (rules 73 [114] [Rule 71 [113] of the present rules of procedure] and 79 [120] [Rule 77 [119] of the present rules of procedure]).

"(b) Points of order raised under rule 73 [114]n involve questions necessitating a ruling by the presiding officer, subject to possible appeal. They are therefore distinct from the procedural motions provided for in rules 76 [117] [Rule 74 [116] of the present rules of procedure] to 79 [120]o which can be decided only by a vote and on which more than one motion may be entertained at the same time, rule 79 [120]o laying down the precedence of such motions. They are also distinct from requests for information or clarification, or from remarks relating to material arrangements (seating, interpretation system, temperature of the room), documents, translations, etc., which - while they may have to be dealt with by the presiding officer - do not require rulings from him. However, in established United Nations practice, a representative intending to submit a procedural motion or to seek information or clarification often rises to 'a point of order' as a means of obtaining the floor. The latter usage, which is based on practical grounds, should not be confused with the raising of points of order under rule 73 [114].

"(c) Under rule 73 [114],n a point of order must be immediately decided by the presiding officer in accordance with the rules of procedure; any appeal arising therefrom must also be put immediately to the vote. It follows that as a general rule:

"(i) A point of order and any appeal arising from a ruling thereon is not debatable;

"(ii) No point of order on the same or a different subject can be permitted until the initial point of order and any appeal arising therefrom have been disposed of.

"Nevertheless, both the presiding officer and delegations may request information or clarification regarding a point of order. In addition, the presiding officer may, if he considers it necessary, request an expression of views from delegations on a point of order before giving his ruling; in the exceptional cases in which this practice is resorted to, the presiding officer should terminate the exchange of views and give his ruling as soon as he is ready to announce that ruling.

"(d) Rule 73 [114]n provides that a representative rising to a point of order may not speak on the substance of the matter under discussion. Consequently, the purely procedural nature of points of order calls for brevity. The presiding officer is responsible for ensuring that statements made on a point of order are in conformity with the present description."

7. Congratulations

80. The Special Committee is of the opinion that it would be better to retain the current practice of the plenary Assembly whereby congratulations to the President are confined to brief remarks included in the speeches made during the general debate [para. 235].

81. With regard to subsidiary organs of the General Assembly, the Special Committee recommends that, in the case of a newly established organ or of the rotation of officers on an existing one, congratulations to the Chairman should be expressed only by the temporary Chairman and congratulations to other officers should be expressed only by the Chairman [para. 237]. [For congratulations in the Main Committees, see rule 110, adopted on the recommendation of the Special Committee].

8. Condolences

82. The Special Committee recommends to the General Assembly that condolences addressed to a delegation on the death of a prominent person or in the event of a disaster should be expressed solely by the President of the General Assembly, by the Chairman of a Main Committee or by the

Chairman of a subsidiary organ on behalf of all members. Where circumstances warrant it, the President of the General Assembly might call a special plenary meeting for that purpose [para. 242].

83. The Special Committee moreover takes note of the practice whereby the President of the General Assembly, on behalf of all members, dispatches a cable to the country concerned [para. 243].

9. Roll-call votes

84. The Special Committee, while believing that there is no need to change the rules of procedure relating to roll-call votes, recommends that delegations should endeavour not to request such a vote except when there are good and sound reasons for doing so [para. 247].

10. Electronic devices

85. The Special Committee did not believe that it should express any views on the possible use of an electronic voting system by all Committees, since the question of the installation of mechanical means of voting was included in the draft agenda of the twenty-sixth session of the General Assembly [para. 249].

86. The Special Committee did not retain the suggestion that a mechanical or electronic timing device might be installed in the General Assembly Hall and the Main Committee rooms [para. 250].

VII. Resolutions

A. Submission of draft resolutions

1. Date of submission of draft resolutions

87. The Special Committee recommends to the General

Assembly that draft resolutions should be submitted as early as possible so as to give debates a more concrete character. It considers, however, that no rigid rule should be established in the matter, since it is for delegations to determine, in each case, the most appropriate moment for submitting draft resolutions [para. 254].

88. So as to ensure that debates take shape as quickly as possible without making it mandatory for delegations to submit a formal draft resolution, the Special Committee also considers that delegations might resort more often to the possibility of circulating draft resolutions as informal working papers which would provide a basis for the discussion but whose contents would be strictly provisional [para. 255].

2. Submission of draft resolutions in writing

89. Because of the appreciable loss of time that such a procedure could entail, the Special Committee decided not to endorse the suggestion that proposals and amendments should be submitted in writing only [para. 256].

3. Consultations

90. The Special Committee, recognizing the indisputable value of consultations, believes that delegations should explore every avenue for arriving at negotiated texts. It considers, however, that the initiative for such consultations must rest solely with the delegations concerned and can, under no circumstances, be dictated in mandatory provisions [para. 258].

91. The Special Committee also believes that the Chairmen of the Main Committees should be invited to bear in mind the possibility of establishing, where necessary, working groups for the purpose of facilitating the adoption

of agreed texts. Such groups may be open, as appropriate, to interested delegations. It does not, however, consider it advisable to contemplate the establishment of such working groups whenever two or more draft resolutions have been introduced on the same matter [para. 259].

4. Number of sponsors

92. The Special Committee did not endorse the suggestion that the number of sponsors of a draft resolution should be limited [para. 260].

93. The Special Committee does, however, wish to draw attention to the practice whereby the sponsors of a proposal decide whether other delegations can become co-sponsors [para. 261].

5. Time-lapse between the submission and the consideration of draft resolutions

94. The Special Committee, while recognizing the difficulties experienced by some delegations in consulting their Governments within the time laid down by rules 80 and 121[Rules 78 and 120 of the present rules of procedure] of the rules of procedure, does not deem it advisable to propose an amendment to those rules [para. 265].

B. Content of Resolutions

95. The Special Committee is of the opinion that the wording of resolutions, to be effective, must be as clear and succinct as possible. It recognizes, however, that only the delegations concerned can decide upon the content of the proposals which they are sponsoring [para. 267].

96. The Special Committee also wishes to emphasize that the text of a draft resolution should not go beyond the

competence of the Committee in which it is submitted. Where, however, it is suggested that a draft resolution does so, the Special Committee feels that it is up to the Committee concerned to take a decision in the matter [para. 268].

C. Financial implications

1. Financial Controls

97. The Special Committee feels that the provisions of rules 154 and 155 [Rules 153 and 154 of the present rules of procedure] of the rules of procedure are satisfactory and should be strictly applied [para. 272].

98. The Special Committee is also of the opinion that the financial implications of draft resolutions should be viewed in terms of an overall assessment of priorities and that the principal organs should give careful consideration to the draft resolutions adopted by their subsidiary organs where such drafts call for the appropriation of funds [para. 273].

2. Work of the Advisory Committee on Administrative and Budgetary Questions

99. The Special Committee recognizes that the Advisory Committee on Administrative and Budgetary Questions should meet more frequently, but does not consider itself qualified to make detailed recommendations on the matter [para. 275].

3. Resolutions setting up new organs

100. While acknowledging that new organs should be set up only after mature consideration, the Special Committee believes that it would be inadvisable to amend the rules of procedure and lay down hard and fast rules in the matter [para. 277].

D. Voting Procedure

1. Required majority

101. The Special Committee considers that rules 88 and 127 [Rules 86 and 126 of the present rules of procedure] of the rules of procedure should be left unchanged [para. 282].

102. The Special Committee also considers that the suggestion referred to in paragraph 279 of the report is unacceptable and, moreover, goes beyond its mandate [para. 283].

2. Measures to accelerate procedures

103. The Special Committee, recalling the recommendations which it has made elsewhere concerning debate on items already considered in Committee (see para. 50 above) and roll-call votes (see para. 84 above), feels that it is inadvisable to make any changes in the relevant provisions of the rules of procedure [para. 287].

3. Consensus

104. The Special Committee considers that the adoption of decisions and resolutions by consensus is desirable when it contributes to the effective and lasting settlement of differences, thus strengthening the authority of the United Nations. It wishes, however, to emphasize that the right of every Member State to set forth its view in full must not be prejudiced by this procedure [para. 289].

E. Reduction in the number of resolutions

105. The Special Committee did not endorse the suggestions aimed at reducing the number of resolutions adopted by the General Assembly [para. 293].

VIII. Documentation

[See also resolution 2836 (XXVI)]

A. Reduction in the volume of documentation

106. The Special Committee recommends that the General Assembly should:

(a) Draw attention to the provisions of its resolutions 2292 (XXII) and 2538 (XXIV) summarized in document A/INF/136, and stress the need for strict adherence to them, not only in letter, but also in spirit, by Member States and also, in the light of its internal rules, by the Secretariat;

(b) Instruct its subsidiary organs to include in the agenda of each session an item on the control and limitation of the documentation of the organ itself in the spirit of paragraph 3 of General Assembly resolution 1272 (XIII) [para. 300].

B. Preparation and distribution of documents

107. The Special Committee recommends to the General Assembly that:

(a) Timely distribution of documents in all working languages should be scrupulously observed;

(b) All the subsidiary organs of the General Assembly should be required to complete their work and submit their reports before the opening of each regular session of the Assembly;

(c) Reports to be considered by the General Assembly should be as brief as possible and contain precise information confined to a description of the work done by the organ concerned, to the conclusions it has reached, to its decisions and to the recommendations made to the Assembly; the reports should include, where appropriate, a summary of proposals, conclusions and recommendations. As a rule, no previously issued material (working papers and other basic documents) should be incorporated in or appended to such reports, but, where necessary, referred to;

(d) Taking into account the needs of Member States, the number of copies of reports and other United Nations documents should, whenever appropriate, be limited, i.e., they should be issued in the /L. series [para. 304]. [For the recommendations concerning the reports of the Main Committees, see para. 43 above]

C. Records of meetings and sound recordings

108. The Special Committee recommends that rule 60, as revised [Rule 58 of the present rules of procedure (see introduction, para. 30 (a))], should be applied in accordance with the following observations:

(a) Summary records should continue to be provided for the General Committee and for all Main Committees other than the First Committee;

(b) The General Assembly, on the recommendation of the General Committee, should decide annually whether the option that has traditionally been approved for the Special Political Committee to have, on specific request, transcriptions of the debates of some of its meetings, or portions thereof, should be maintained;

(c) The provision of summary records to subsidiary organs should be reviewed periodically by the General Assembly in the light of the report of the Joint Inspection Unit on the use of minutes instead of summary records, and of the comments of the Secretary-General and the Advisory Committee on Administrative and Budgetary Questions thereon [E/4802 and Add.1 and Add.2];

(d) Sound recordings should be kept by the Secretariat in accordance with its practice [para. 309].

IX. Subsidiary Organs of the General Assembly

A. Reduction of the number of organs

109. The Special Committee recommends that the General Assembly should review, either periodically or when considering their reports, the usefulness of its various subsidiary organs [para. 313].

110. The Special Committee also recommends that the General Assembly should consider the possibility of merging some of these organs [para. 314].

B. Composition of organs

111. The Special Committee considers that membership of a body depends on the nature and function of that body and that it cannot, therefore, be subject to any general rule [para. 318].

112. The Special Committee is of the opinion that subsidiary organs of the General Assembly should, where appropriate, have the authority to invite a Member State which is not a member of the organ concerned to participate without vote in the discussion of a matter which the organ considers to be of particular interest to that Member State [para. 319].

113. The Special Committee is also of the opinion that the composition of subsidiary organs should be subject to periodic change [para. 320].

114. Finally, the Special Committee considers that visits of subsidiary organs away from their normal meeting places should be authorized by the General Assembly only when the nature of the work renders such visits essential [para. 321].

C. Calendar of meetings

115. The Special Committee recommends to the General Assembly that the Secretary-General should play a greater role in drawing up the calendar of meetings, it being understood that in every case the final decision rests with the organ concerned [para. 323].

X. Other Questions

A. Credentials of delegations

116. The Special Committee, while aware of the problems posed by the non-recognition by the General Assembly of a delegation's credentials, feels that it is not in a position to make any proposal on the matter [para. 327].

B. Role of the Secretary-General

117. The Special Committee is of the opinion that the Secretary-General should play an active role in making suggestions with regard to the organization of sessions, it being understood that the final decision on the recommendations he makes lies with the General Assembly [para. 331].

C. Secretariat

118. The Special Committee considers that the question of the reorganization of the Secretariat, however valid it might be, does not come within its terms of reference. It is of the opinion, therefore, that it should not make any recommendation on the matter [para. 333].

D. Guidance regarding General Assembly procedure and assistance to presiding officers

1. Preparation of a manual on procedure

119. The Special Committee recommends that the General Assembly should consider requesting the Secretary-General to prepare a systematic and comprehensive compilation

of the conclusions which the Assembly may adopt on the basis of the reports of the Special Committee and of the Joint Inspection Unit, this compilation to form an annex to the rules of procedure of the General Assembly [para. 339].

2. Repertory of Practice of United Nations Organs

120. The Special Committee, recognizing the usefulness of the Repertory of Practice of United Nations Organs, expresses the hope that it will be brought up to date as quickly as possible [para. 341].

3. Preparation of a repertory of practice on the rules of procedure of the General Assembly

121. The Special Committee did not consider that it should endorse the proposal to issue a repertory of practice on the rules of procedure of the General Assembly [para. 344].

4. Reminders of previous recommendations

122. It was suggested that at the beginning of the session the President of the General Assembly should remind the Assembly of, and particularly invite the attention of the Chairmen of Main Committees to, the recommendations for improving the methods of work which were specifically approved in General Assembly resolution 1898 (XVIII) [See annex III]. While there was general agreement on the principle underlying that suggestion, the Special Committee did not feel that it need make any specific recommendation in that regard [paras. 345 and 346].

123. The Special Committee did not retain the suggestion that the report of the Ad Hoc Committee on the Improvement of the Methods of Work of the General Assembly [Official Records of the General Assembly, Eighteenth Session, Annexes, agenda item 25, document A/

5423] should be reissued on account of the financial implications that such a measure would entail [paras. 345 and 346].

5. Assistance in procedural matters

124. The Special Committee noted that it was not possible to assign a member of the Office of Legal Affairs continuously to each of the Main Committees but that legal advice was always furnished, either orally or in writing, when requested [para. 348].

125. The Special Committee did not consider that it should make any recommendation on the proposal that the President of the General Assembly and the Chairmen of Main Committees should enlist several assistants under them, both from the Secretariat and, wherever possible, from the delegations themselves, to whom they would allocate items on the agenda for the purpose of closely following them up with the delegations directly concerned and expediting the progress of the General Assembly [paras. 347 and 348].

E. Studies of the rules of procedure

126. The Special Committee did not consider that it should retain the suggestions concerning the insertion in the rules of procedure of the General Assembly of provisions similar to those in the rules of procedure of the Economic and Social Council [para. 352].

127. The Special Committee took note of the proposal concerning a comparative study of the rules of procedure of the General Assembly and those of the governing bodies of the specialized agencies and suggests that the United Nations Institute for Training and Research should consider undertaking such a project [para. 353].

128. Lastly, the Special Committee recommends to the General Assembly that the Secretariat should be instructed to undertake a comparative study of the versions of the General Assembly's rules of procedure in the various official languages in order to ensure their concordance [para. 354].

F. Special training programme

129. The Special Committee, aware of the training problems facing delegations, particularly as regards newly arrived representatives, suggests that the United Nations Institute for Training and Research should consider ways of helping to solve these problems [para. 356].

G. Regional groups

130. The Special Committee endorses the suggestion that the names of chairmen of the regional groups for the month should be published in the Journal of the United Nations and recommends that it should be left to the Secretariat to decide how often it should be applied [paras. 357 and 358].

Annex V

Decision 34/401 on the rationalization of the procedures and organization of the General Assembly (a)

I. Organization of the Session

A. General Committee

1. The General Committee should, at the outset of each session, consider how the work of the session can best be rationalized.
2. The General Committee should also meet periodically throughout the session to review the progress of work and to make recommendations to the General Assembly

on the general programme of the session and on measures aimed at improving its work.

B. Schedule of meetings

3. Both plenary and committee meetings should begin at 10.30 a.m. and 3 p.m. and, in order to expedite the work of the General Assembly, all meetings should begin promptly at the scheduled time.

C. Allocation of items

4. Substantive items should normally be discussed initially in a Main Committee and, therefore, items previously allocated to plenary meetings should henceforth be referred to a Main Committee unless there are compelling circumstances requiring their continued consideration in plenary meeting.

D. General debate

5. Out of consideration for the other speakers and in order to preserve the dignity of the general debate, delegations should refrain from expressing their congratulations in the General Assembly Hall after a speech has been delivered.

E. Explanations of vote

6. Explanations of vote should be limited to ten minutes.

7. When the same draft resolution is considered in a Main Committee and in plenary meeting, a delegation should, as far as possible, explain its vote only once, i.e., either in the Committee or in plenary meeting, unless that delegation's vote in plenary meeting is different from its vote in the Committee.

F. Right of reply

8. Delegations should exercise their right of reply at the end of the day whenever two meetings have been

scheduled for that day and whenever such meetings are devoted to the consideration of the same item.

9. The number of interventions in the exercise of the right of reply for any delegation at a given meeting should be limited to two per item.

10. The first intervention in the exercise of the right of reply for any delegation on any item at a given meeting should be limited to ten minutes and the second intervention should be limited to five minutes.

G. Non-utilization of the rostrum

11. Explanations of vote, interventions in the exercise of the right of reply and procedural motions should be made by delegations from their seats.

H. Budgetary and financial questions

12. It is imperative that Main Committees should allow sufficient time for the preparation of the estimate of expenditures by the Secretariat and for its consideration by the Advisory Committee on Administrative and Budgetary Questions and the Fifth Committee and that they should take this requirement into account when they adopt their programme of work.

13. Furthermore:

(a) A mandatory deadline, not later than 1 December, should be established for the submission to the Fifth Committee of all draft resolutions with financial implications;

(b) The Fifth Committee should, as a general practice, consider accepting without debate the recommendations of the Advisory Committee on Administrative and Budgetary Questions on the financial implications of draft resolutions up to a prescribed limit, namely, $25,000 on any one item;

(c) Firm deadlines should be set for the early submission

of the reports of subsidiary organs which require consideration by the Fifth Committee;

(d) A minimum period of forty-eight hours should be allowed between the submission and the voting of a proposal involving expenditure in order to allow the Secretary-General to prepare and present the related statement of administrative and financial implications.

I. Reports of the Main Committees

14. Reports of the Main Committees should be as concise as possible and, save in exceptional cases, should not contain a summary of the debates.

15. The practice of dealing in plenary meeting with reports of the Second Committee, whereby it is stated that the positions of delegations regarding draft resolutions recommended by the Second Committee have been made clear in the Committee and are reflected in the relevant official records, should be extended to reports of other committees.

J. Balloting procedure

16. The practice of dispensing with the secret ballot for elections to subsidiary organs when the number of candidates corresponds to the number of seats to be filled should become standard and the same practice should apply to the election of the President and Vice-Presidents of the General Assembly, unless a delegation specifically requests a vote on a given election.

K. Concluding statements

17. To save time at the end of the session, the practice of making concluding statements in the General Assembly and its Main Committees should be dispensed with except for statements by the presiding officers.

II. Work of the Main Committees

18. Before the conclusion of a session of the General Assembly, regional groups should agree on the distribution of chairmanships among them for the following session.
19. Candidates for the chairmanships of the Main Committees should be nominated as soon as possible.
20. It is strongly recommended that nominees for the chairmanships of the Main Committees should have experience in the work of the General Assembly.
21. During sessions, the Chairmen or other officers of the Main Committees should be entrusted by their Committees, whenever appropriate, with the conduct of informal negotiations aimed at reaching agreement on specific issues.
22. Chairmen of Main Committees should fully exercise their authority under rule 106 of the rules of procedure and, in particular, propose more frequently the limitation of the time to be allowed to speakers or of the number of times each representative may speak on any given item.
23. The Main Committees which require the largest number of meetings should be encouraged to hold more meetings early in the session in order to ensure a better distribution of meetings over the whole session.

III. Documentation

24. Subsidiary organs should be required to complete their work at the latest by 1 September, so that their reports may be available in all the working languages in time for consideration by the opening of the session of the General Assembly, and the Committee on Conferences should take this provision fully into account.
25. No reports should contain a compilation of other previous documents.

26. Subsidiary organs should not annex to their reports summary records of their meetings or other material which were already distributed to all Member States.
27. The General Assembly should review periodically the need for summary records of its subsidiary organs.
28. The General Assembly, including its Main Committees, should merely take note of those reports of the Secretary-General or subsidiary organs which do not require a decision by the Assembly and should neither debate nor adopt resolutions on them, unless specifically requested to do so by the Secretary-General or the organ concerned.
29. The publication of reports of the principal organs and of subsidiary organs of the General Assembly and of draft resolutions and amendments should be given priority over that of any individual communications received from Member States.
30. Member States should refrain, to the extent possible, from requesting the circulation of any individual communications as documents of the General Assembly and in lieu thereof, where circulation of such documents is desired, should, as far as possible, request such circulation under the cover of a note verbale in the official languages in which they submit them.

IV. Resolutions

31. Subsidiary organs reporting to the General Assembly should make every effort to submit draft resolutions in order to facilitate the consideration of the items.
32. Whenever possible, resolutions requesting the discussion of a question at a subsequent session should not call

for the inclusion of a separate new item and such discussion should be held under the item under which the resolution was adopted.

V. Planning of Meetings

33. The Committee on Conferences should be authorized to play a more effective role in the planning of meetings and in the use of conference facilities.

34. No subsidiary organ of the General Assembly should be permitted to meet at United Nations Headquarters during a regular session of the Assembly, unless explicitly authorized by the Assembly.

VI. Subsidiary Organs of the General Assembly

[This section, which related mostly to the establishment of the Ad Hoc Committee on Subsidiary Organs, has not been reproduced in the present annex]...

Rules of Procedure

Annex VI A

Conclusions of the Special Committee on the Charter of the United Nations and on the Strengthening of the Role of the Organization concerning the rationalization of the procedures of the General Assembly (a)

1. The agenda of the sessions of the General Assembly should be simplified as much as possible by grouping or merging related items, after consultation and with the agreement of the delegations concerned. [The view was expressed that the agreement of the delegations concerned was not an essential condition.]

2. Specific items should be referred, where relevant, to other United Nations organs or to specialized agencies. The right of States to request that specific items be discussed

in the General Assembly should remain unimpaired.

3. The recommendation in paragraph 28 of annex IV to the rules of procedure of the General Assembly, according to which the Assembly should ensure, as far as possible, that the same questions, or the same aspects of a question, are not considered by more than one Main Committee, should be more fully implemented, except when it would be helpful for the Sixth Committee to be consulted on the legal aspects of questions under consideration by other Main Committees.
4. The General Committee should play more fully its role under rule 42 of the rules of procedure and paragraphs 1 and 2 of General Assembly decision 34/401, reviewing periodically the work of the Assembly and making the necessary recommendations.
5. The Chairmen of the Main Committees should take the initiative, in the light of past experience, to propose the grouping of similar or related items and the holding of a single general debate on them.
6. The Chairmen of the Main Committees should propose to the Committee the closing of the list of speakers on each item at a suitably early stage.
7. Agreed programmes of work should be respected. To this end, meetings should start at the scheduled time and the time allotted for meetings should be fully utilized.
8. The officers of each Main Committee should review periodically the progress of work. In case of need, they should propose appropriate measures to ensure that the work remains on schedule.
9. Negotiation procedures should be carefully selected to suit the particular subject matter.
10. The Secretariat should facilitate informal consultations

by providing adequate conference services. [The view was expressed that the agreement of the delegations concerned was not an essential condition.]

11. The mandate of subsidiary organs should be carefully defined in order to avoid overlapping and duplication of work. The General Assembly should also review periodically the usefulness of its subsidiary organs.

12. Resolutions should be as clear and succinct as possible.

Annex VII (A)

Conclusions of the Special Committee on the Charter of the United Nations and on the Strengthening of the Role of the Organization concerning the rationalization of existing United Nations procedures

1. Without prejudice to Article 18 of the Charter of the United Nations and with a view to facilitating the work of the United Nations, including, whenever possible, the adoption by the General Assembly of agreed texts of resolutions and decisions, informal consultations should be carried out with the widest possible participation of Member States.
2. When an electronic voting system is available for recording how votes were cast, a roll-call vote should as far as possible not be requested.
3. Before the end of each session of the General Assembly, the General Committee should, in the light of the experience it has acquired during that session, consider drawing up its observations on the organization of the work of the session, with a view to facilitating the organization of the work of future sessions of the General Assembly.
4. The agenda of the General Assembly should be simplified

by grouping or merging, to the extent possible, related items and, where it is appropriate for discussion of a particular item, by setting an interval of more than a year between the discussions on it. For this purpose, the Chairman of the Main Committee concerned or, as appropriate, the President of the General Assembly, should undertake consultations with delegations.

5. The General Committee should consider, at the beginning of each session of the General Assembly, recommending that certain Main Committees should meet in sequential order, taking into account such matters as the number of meetings required for the consideration of the questions with which they are charged at that session, the organization of the work of the whole session and the problem of participation of smaller delegations.
6. In making recommendations as to how agenda items should be allocated to the Main Committees and to the plenary Assembly, the General Committee should ensure the best use of the expertise of the Committees.
7. When the General Assembly considers whether it needs to establish subsidiary organs, in accordance with Article 22 of the Charter, it should give careful consideration as to whether the subject matter in question could be dealt with by existing organs, including its Main Committees and their working groups. Subsidiary organs should seek constantly to improve their procedures and methods of work in order to ensure effective consideration of questions allocated to them by the Assembly.
8. The dates and length of the sessions of bodies of the General Assembly that meet intersessionally should be determined as soon as possible by the Assembly, as appropriate, following advice from the Committee on

Conferences, on the proposal of the Secretary-General. The Assembly should take account of the past experience, the state of current work in regard to the mandate given to the body in question and the need to avoid as far as possible overlapping meetings of bodies that deal with subject matter of a similar nature.

9. Informal consultations about the work of bodies of the General Assembly that meet intersessionally should continue to be held in advance of the sessions of such bodies in order to facilitate the conduct of their sessions, especially as regards the composition of the bureau and the organization of work.

10. Resolutions should request observations from States or reports by the Secretary-General insofar as they are likely to facilitate the implementation of the resolutions or the continued examination of the question.

Annex VIII (A)

Guidelines on the Rationalization of the Agenda of the General Assembly

1. The plenary meetings of the General Assembly should constitute a forum for high-level policy statements, as well as for the consideration, inter alia, of agenda items of special political importance and/or urgency.

2. Agenda items which are of a nature that relates to more than one Main Committee or which do not come within the purview of any Main Committee should be considered by the General Assembly in plenary meeting, taking into account the recommendations of the General Committee.

3. Substantive items initially allocated directly to a plenary meeting of the General Assembly could be reviewed for allocation to a Main Committee in accordance with

the rules of procedure of the Assembly, in particular with Assembly decision 34/401, which is reproduced in annex VI to the rules of procedure.

4. There shall be periodic reviews of the agenda, taking into account the views of concerned Member States, in order to ascertain whether it is possible to delete any item on which no resolution or decision has been adopted for a period of time.

5. The Main Committees should be encouraged to continue with the review of their respective agendas, taking into account, inter alia, the following:

(*a*) Agenda items concerning issued of closely related substance could be merged within a single agenda title or be incorporated as sub-items where this is possible without loss of focus on the items/sub-items concerned;

(*b*) Items that cover related matters or issued could be considered in agreed clusters;

(*c*) Biennialization and triennialization of items on the agenda of the Main Committees could be considered in accordance with the relevant resolutions of the General Assembly;

(*d*) The existing broad division of work among the Main Committees should be maintained.

Annex IX (A)

Opening date and duration of the general debate

"*The General Assembly,* ...

"2. *Also decides* that the general debate in the General Assembly shall open on the Tuesday following the opening of the regular session of the General Assembly and shall be held without interruption over a period of nine working days".

4

United Nations Security Council

The United Nations Security Council (UNSC) is the organ of the United Nations charged with the maintenance of international peace and security. Its powers, outlined in the United Nations Charter, include the establishment of peacekeeping operations, the establishment of international sanctions regimes, and the authorization for military action. Its powers are exercised through United Nations Security Council Resolutions.

History

The Security Council held its first session on 17 January 1946 at Church House, London.

Since its first meeting, the Council, which exists in continuous session, has traveled widely, holding meetings in many cities, such as Paris and Addis Ababa. For the most part, however, it has remained located at UN Headquarters — first at Lake Success in New York and then at its current home in New York City.

Significant changes in the Council's composition have occurred on three occasions. In 1965, amendments to articles 23 and 27 of the Charter came into effect, increasing the number of elected members from six to ten.

In 1971, the General Assembly voted to remove the Republic of China representative, establishing that a delegate from the People's Republic of China was the legitimate representative of China. Because the issue was presented as one that involved which delegation would properly represent China instead of admission or expulsion of a member, this issue required only action by the General Assembly. Under typical circumstances, removal of a member from the Council requires endorsement from Council itself, or the amendment to article 23 that specifies the identity of the permanent members on the Council.

Similarly, there was no amendment to article 23 following the collapse of the Union of Soviet Socialist Republics in 1991. In much less contentious circumstances the Russian Federation acceded to the former Soviet seat.

Members

The basic structure of the UNSC is set out in Chapter V of the UN Charter.

Security Council members must always be present at UN headquarters in New York so that the Security Council can meet at any time. This requirement of the United Nations Charter was adopted to address a weakness of the League of Nations since that organization was often unable to respond quickly to a crisis.

The role of president of the Security Council involves

setting the agenda, presiding at its meetings and overseeing any crisis. It rotates in alphabetical order of the Security Council member nations' names in English.

There are two categories of membership in the UN Security Council: permanent members and elected members.

Permanent Members

The Council seated five permanent members who were originally drawn from the victorious powers after World War II:

- The French Republic
- The Republic of China
- The Union of Soviet Socialist Republics
- The United Kingdom of Great Britain and Northern Ireland
- The United States of America

Two of the original members, the Republic of China and the Soviet Union, were later replaced by recognized successor states, even though Article 23 of the Charter of the United Nations has not been accordingly amended:

- The People's Republic of China
- The Russian Federation

Since the stalemate of the Chinese Civil War, there have been two states claiming to represent "China" and thus both officially claim each other's territory. In 1971, the People's Republic of China was awarded China's seat in the United Nations by UN General Assembly Resolution 2758, and the Republic of China (which had lost mainland China and been in Taiwan since 1949) soon lost membership in all

UN organizations. In 1991, Russia, being the legal successor state to the Soviet Union, acquired the originally-Soviet seat, including the Soviet Union's former representation in the Security Council.

The five permanent members of the Security Council are the only nations recognized as possessing nuclear weapons under the Nuclear Non-Proliferation Treaty, although it lacks universal validity, as some nuclear nations have not signed the treaty. This nuclear status is not the result of their Security Council membership, though it is sometimes used as a modern-day justification for their continued presence on the body. India , Pakistan and North Korea possess nuclear weapons outside of the anti-proliferation framework established by the Treaty. Israel does not officially confirm or deny having nuclear weapons, but is generally believed to .

In 2004, four of the five permanent members were also the world's top four weapons exporters when measured by arms value; China was seventh.

Each permanent member has the power to veto any substantive resolution. (See Veto power, below.)

The Permanent Representatives of the U.N. Security Council permanent members are Wang Guangya, Jean-Maurice Ripert, Vitaly Churkin, John Sawers and Zalmay Khalilzad.

Elected Members

Ten other members are elected by the General Assembly for two-year terms starting on 1 January, with five replaced each year. The members are chosen by regional groups and confirmed by the United Nations General Assembly. The African bloc chooses three members; the Latin America and the Caribbean, Asian, and Western European and Others blocs choose two members each; and the Eastern European bloc chooses one member. Also, one of these members is an Arab country, alternately from the Asian or African bloc.

The current (2008) elected members, with the regions they were elected to represent and their Permanent Representatives, are:

Country	Regional bloc(s)	Ambassador
Belgium	Western Europe and Other	Jan Grauls
Burkina Faso	Africa	Michel Kafando
Costa Rica	Latin America and Caribbean	Jorge Urbina Ortega
Croatia	Eastern Europe	Neven Jurica
Indonesia	Asia	Marty Natalegawa
Italy	Western Europe and Other	Marcello Spatafora
Libya	Africa, Arab	Jadallah Azzuz at-Talhi
Panama	Latin America and Caribbean	Ricardo Alberto Arias
South Africa	Africa	Dumisani Kumalo
Vietnam	Asia	Lê Lýõng Minh

Until 2000 Israel was the only United Nations member country not a member of any regional group and so could not be elected to the Security Council or become involved in many consultative UN bodies. Israel would normally fall within the Asia group but many Arab states blocked Israel's inclusion in this group. In 2000 Israel was granted temporary membership in the Western European and Others Group

(WEOG) and this was extended indefinitely in 2004. Israel is limited in the activities that it can undertake as part of WEOG.

Veto Power

Under Article 27 of the UN Charter, Security Council decisions on all substantive matters require the affirmative votes of nine members. A negative vote, or *veto*, by a permanent member prevents adoption of a proposal, even if it has received the required number of affirmative votes. Abstention is not regarded as a veto despite the wording of the Charter. Since the Security Council's inception, China (ROC/PRC) has used its veto 6 times; France 18 times; Russia/USSR 122 times; the United Kingdom 32 times; and the United States 81 times. The majority of Russian/Soviet vetoes were in the first ten years of the Council's existence. Since 1984, China (ROC/PRC) has vetoed three resolutions; France three; Russia/USSR four; the United Kingdom ten; and the United States 43.

Procedural matters are not subject to a veto, so the veto cannot be used to avoid discussion of an issue.

Status of Non-members

A state that is a member of the UN, but not of the Security Council, may participate in Security Council discussions in matters by which the Council agrees that the country's interests are particularly affected. In recent years, the Council has interpreted this loosely, allowing many countries to take part in its discussions. Non-members are routinely invited to take part when they are parties to disputes being considered by the Council.

Role of the Security Council

Under Chapter Six of the Charter, "Pacific Settlement of Disputes", the Security Council "may investigate any dispute, or any situation which might lead to international friction or give rise to a dispute". The Council may "recommend appropriate procedures or methods of adjustment" if it determines that the situation might endanger international peace and security. These recommendations are not binding on UN members.

Under Chapter Seven, the Council has broader power to decide what measures are to be taken in situations involving "threats to the peace, breaches of the peace, or acts of aggression". In such situations, the Council is not limited to recommendations but may take action, including the use of armed force "to maintain or restore international peace and security". This was the basis for UN armed action in Korea in 1950 during the Korean War and the use of coalition forces in Iraq and Kuwait in 1991. Decisions taken under Chapter Seven, such as economic sanctions, are binding on UN members.

The UN's role in international collective security is defined by the UN Charter, which gives the Security Council the power to:

- Investigate any situation threatening international peace;
- Recommend procedures for peaceful resolution of a dispute;
- Call upon other member nations to completely or partially interrupt economic relations as well as sea, air, postal, and radio communications, or to sever diplomatic relations; and
- Enforce its decisions militarily, or by any means necessary.

The United Nations has helped prevent many outbreaks of international violence from growing into wider conflicts. It has opened the way to negotiated settlements through its service as a centre of debate and negotiation, as well as through UN-sponsored fact-finding missions, mediators, and truce observers. UN Peacekeeping forces, made up of troops and equipment supplied by member nations, have usually been able to limit or prevent conflict, although sometimes not. Some conflicts, however, have proven to be beyond the capacity of the UN to influence. Key to the success of UN peacekeeping efforts is the willingness of the parties to a conflict to come to terms peacefully through a viable political process.

The Rome Statute of the International Criminal Court recognizes that the Security Council has authority to refer cases to the Court, where the Court could not otherwise exercise jurisdiction. The Council exercised this power for the first time in March 2005, when it referred to the Court "the situation prevailing in Darfur since 1 July 2002"; since Sudan is not a party to the Rome Statute, the Court could not otherwise have exercised jurisdiction.

Responsibility to Protect

UN Security Council Resolution 1674, adopted by the United Nations Security Council on 28 April 2006, "reaffirms the provisions of paragraphs 138 and 139 of the 2005 World Summit Outcome Document regarding the responsibility to protect populations from genocide, war crimes, ethnic cleansing and crimes against humanity". The resolution commits the Council to action to protect civilians in armed conflict.

Resolutions

Security Council Resolutions are legally binding if they are made under Chapter VII (*Action with Respect to Threats to the Peace, Breaches of the Peace, and Acts of Aggression*) of the Charter. Resolutions made under Chapter VI (*Pacific Settlement of Disputes*), however, have no enforcement mechanisms and are generally considered to have no binding force under international law. In 1971, however, a majority of the then International Court of Justice (ICJ) members asserted in the non-binding *Namibia* advisory opinion that all UN Security Council resolutions are legally binding. This assertion by the ICJ has been countered by Erika De Wet and others. De Wet argues that Chapter VI resolutions *cannot* be binding. Her reasoning, in part states:

> Allowing the Security Council to adopt binding measures under Chapter VI would undermine the structural division of competencies foreseen by Chapters VI and VII, respectively. The whole aim of separating these chapters is to distinguish between voluntary and binding measures. Whereas the pacific settlement of disputes provided by the former is underpinned by the consent of the parties, binding measures in terms of Chapter VII are characterised by the absence of such consent. A further indication of the non-binding nature of measures taken in terms of Chapter VI is the obligation on members of the Security Council who are parties to a dispute, to refrain from voting when resolutions under Chapter VI are adopted. No similar obligation exists with respect to binding resolutions adopted under Chapter VII... If one applies this reasoning to the *Namibia* opinion, the decisive point is that none of the Articles under Chapter VI facilitate the adoption of the type of binding measures

that were adopted by the Security Council in Resolution 276(1970)... Resolution 260(1970) was indeed adopted in terms of Chapter VII, even though the ICJ went to some length to give the opposite impression.

In practice, the Security Council does not consider its decisions outside Chapter VII to be binding.

Those resolutions made outside these two Chapters dealing with the internal governance of the organization (such as the admission of new Member States) are legally binding where the Charter gives the Security Council power to make them.

If the council cannot reach consensus or a passing vote on a resolution, they may choose to produce a non-binding presidential statement instead of a Resolution. These are adopted by consensus. They are meant to apply political pressure — a warning that the council is paying attention and further action may follow.

Press statements typically accompany both resolutions and presidential statements, carrying the text of the document adopted by the body and also some explanatory text. They may also be released independently, after a significant meeting.

Criticisms of the Security Council

There have been criticisms that the five permanent members of the United Nations Security Council (who are all nuclear powers) have created an exclusive nuclear club whose powers are unchecked. Unlike the General Assembly, which has true international representation, the United Nations Security Council does not. This has led to accusations that the UNSC only addresses the strategic interests and political motives of the permanent members, especially in humanitarian interventions - for example, protecting the oil-rich Kuwaitis in 1991 but poorly protecting resource-poor Rwandans in 1994. Any nation may be elected to serve a temporary term on the Security Council, but critics have suggested this is inadequate. Rather, they argue, the number of permanent members should be expanded to include non-nuclear powers, which would democratize the organization. Still other nations have advocated abolishing the concept of permanency altogether; under the government of Paul Martin, Canada advocated this approach.

Another criticism of the Security Council involves the veto power of the five permanent nations. As it stands, a veto from any of the permanent members can halt any possible action the Council may take. One nation's objection, rather than the opinions of a majority of nations, may cripple any possible UN armed or diplomatic response to a crisis. For instance, John J. Mearsheimer claimed that "Since 1982, the US has vetoed 32 Security Council resolutions critical of Israel, more than the total number of vetoes cast by all the other Security Council members." The practice of the permanent members meeting privately and then presenting their resolutions to the full council as a fait accompli has also drawn fire; according to Erskine Childers, "the vast majority of members — North as well as South — have made very clear...their distaste for the way three Western powers behave in the Council, like a private club of hereditary elite-members who secretly come to decisions and then emerge to tell the grubby elected members that they may now rubber-stamp those decisions."

Other critics and even proponents of the Security Council question its effectiveness and relevance because in most high profile cases, there are essentially no consequences for violating a Security Council resolution. The most prominent and dramatic example of this became the Darfur crisis, in which Arab Janjaweed militias, supported by the Sudanese government, committed repeated acts of ethnic cleansing and genocide against the indigenous population. Thus far, an estimated 300,000 civilians have been killed in what is the largest case of mass murder in the history of the region, yet the U.N. has continuously failed to act against this severe and ongoing human rights issue. Another such case occurred in the Srebrenica massacre where Serbian troops committed genocide against Bosnian Muslims in the largest case of mass murder on the European continent since World War II. Srebrenica had been declared a U.N. "safe area" and was even protected by 400 armed Dutch peacekeepers, but the U.N. forces did nothing to prevent the massacre.

Other critics object to the idea that the U.N. is a democratic organization, saying that it represents the interests of the governments of the nations who form it and not necessarily the individuals within those nations. World federalist Dieter Heinrich points out that the powerful Security Council system does not have distinctions between the legislative, executive, and judiciary branches: the UN Charter gives all three powers to the Security Council.

Membership Reform

There has been discussion of increasing the number of permanent members. The countries who have made the strongest demands for permanent seats are Brazil, Germany,

India and Japan. Indeed, Japan and Germany are the UN's second and third largest funders respectively, while Brazil, the largest Latin American nation, and India, the world's largest democracy and second most populous country, are two of the largest contributors of troops to UN-mandated peace-keeping missions. This project has found opposition in a group of countries called Uniting for Consensus.

Former UN Secretary-General Kofi Annan asked a team of advisors to come up with recommendations for reforming the United Nations by the end of 2004. One proposed measure is to increase the number of permanent members by five, which, in most proposals, would include Brazil, Germany, India, Japan (known as the G4 nations), one seat from Africa (most likely between Egypt, Nigeria or South Africa) and/or one seat from the Arab League. On 21 September 2004, the G4 nations issued a joint statement mutually backing each other's claim to permanent status, together with two African countries. Currently the proposal has to be accepted by two-thirds of the General Assembly (128 votes).

Chamber

The designated Security Council Chamber in the United Nations Conference Building, designed by the Norwegian architect Arnstein Arneberg, was the specific gift of Norway. The mural painted by the Norwegian artist Per Krogh depicts a phoenix rising from its ashes, symbolic of the world reborn after World War II. In the blue and gold silk tapestry on the walls and in the draperies of the windows overlooking the East River appear the anchor of faith, the wheat stems of hope, and the heart of charity.

The Security Council has primary responsibility, under the Charter,for the maintenance of international peace and security. It is so organized as to be able to function continuously, and a representative of each of its members must be present at all times at United Nations Headquarters. On 31 January 1992, the first ever Summit Meeting of the Council was convened at Headquarters, attended by Heads of State and Government of 13 of its 15 members and by the Ministers for Foreign Affairs of the remaining two. The Council may meet elsewhere than at Headquarters; in 1972, it held a session in Addis Ababa, Ethiopia, and the following year in Panama City, Panama.

When a complaint concerning a threat to peace is brought before it, the Council's first action is usually to recommend to the parties to try to reach agreement by peaceful means. In some cases, the Council itself undertakes investigation and mediation. It may appoint special representatives or request the Secretary-General to do so or to use his good offices. It may set forth principles for a peaceful settlement.

When a dispute leads to fighting, the Council's first concern is to bring it to an end as soon as possible. On many occasions, the Council has issued cease-fire directives which have been instrumental in preventing wider hostilities. It also sends United Nations peace-keeping forces to help reduce tensions in troubled areas, keep opposing forces apart and create conditions of calm in which peaceful settlements may be sought. The Council may decide on enforcement measures, economic sanctions (such as trade embargoes) or collective military action.

A Member State against which preventive or enforcement action has been taken by the Security Council may be suspended from the exercise of the rights and privileges of membership by the General Assembly on the recommendation of the Security Council. A Member State which has persistently violated the principles of the Charter may be expelled from the United Nations by the Assembly on the Council's recommendation.

A State which is a Member of the United Nations but not of the Security Council may participate, without a vote, in its discussions when the Council considers that that country's interests are affected. Both Members of the United Nations and non-members, if they are parties to a dispute being considered by the Council, are invited to take part, without a vote, in the Council's discussions; the Council sets the conditions for participation by a non-member State.

The Presidency of the Council rotates monthly, according to the English alphabetical listing of its member States.

Under the Charter, the functions and powers of the Security Council are:

- to maintain international peace and security in accordance with the principles and purposes of the United Nations;
- to investigate any dispute or situation which mightlead to international friction;
- to recommend methods of adjusting such disputes or the terms of settlement;
- to formulate plans for the establishment of a system to regulate armaments;

- to determine the existence of a threat to the peace or act of aggression and to recommend what action should be taken;
- to call on Members to apply economic sanctions and other measures not involving the use of force to prevent or stop aggression;
- to take military action against an aggressor;
- to recommend the admission of new Members;
- to exercise the trusteeship functions of the United Nations in "strategic areas";
- to recommend to the GeneralAssembly the appointment of the Secretary-General and, together with the Assembly, to elect the Judges of the International Court of Justice.

5

United Nations Economic and Social Council

The Economic and Social Council (ECOSOC) of the United Nations assists the General Assembly in promoting international economic and social cooperation and development. ECOSOC has 54 members, all of whom are elected by the General Assembly for a three-year term. The president is elected for a one-year term and chosen amongst the small or middle powers represented on ECOSOC. ECOSOC meets once a year in July for a four-week session. Since 1998, it has held another meeting each April with finance ministers heading key committees of the World Bank and the International Monetary Fund (IMF). Viewed separate from the specialized bodies it coordinates, ECOSOC's functions include information gathering, advising member nations, and making recommendations. In addition, ECOSOC is well positioned to provide policy coherence and coordinate the overlapping functions of the UN's subsidiary bodies and it is in these roles that it is most active.

President of ECOSOC

The current president of ECOSOC is Leo Merores, of

Haiti. The president is elected for a one-year term and chosen amongst the small or middle powers represented on ECOSOC.

Reform

Amendments to the United Nations Charter altered Chapter X to expand ECOSOC from 18 to 27 members in 1965, and to 54 members in 1971.

Through much of its history, ECOSOC has served primarily as a discussion vehicle for economic and social issues. ECOSOC had little authority to force action and a number of member states were concerned that its utility was only marginal. However, beginning in 1992, the US and other nations began an effort to make ECOSOC more relevant by strengthening its policy responsibilities in economic, social, and related fields, particularly in furthering development objectives.

The resulting reform made ECOSOC the oversight and policy-setting body for UN operational development activities and established smaller executive boards for the UN Development Programme (UNDP), UN Population Fund (UNFPA), and UN Children's Fund (UNICEF), which would provide those agencies with operating guidance and promote more effective management. The reform also gave ECOSOC a strong hand in ensuring that UN agencies coordinated their work on issues of common interest, such as narcotics control, human rights, the alleviation of poverty, and the prevention of HIV/AIDS.

One positive impact of this reform was the manner in which the UN development system began to respond more coherently and efficiently to humanitarian crises around the world. Secretary General Annan's recent reform initiatives have attached considerable importance to further strengthening coordination among relief agencies.

Another example was the ECOSOC decision in 1994 to authorize the creation of a new joint and cosponsored UN program on HIV/AIDS. This program (UNAIDS) will bring together the existing AIDS-related resources and expertise of the World Health Organization, UNICEF, UNDP, UNFPA, UNESCO, and the World Bank into one consolidated global program, eliminating duplication of effort and enhancing the ability of member states to cope with the AIDS pandemic. It began operating in January 1996.

ECOSOC Resolution 1996/31 allows for the roughly 2000 NGOs holding consultative status to have input "into ECOSOC's deliberations" including public meetings, UN international conferences, and "to place items on the agendas of ECOSOC and its subsidiary bodies", and to present statements to governments.

A new function of the Economic and Social Council is the Annual Ministerial Review (AMR). This was the result of the 2005 World Summit attended by Heads of State and Government. Through this review, the ECOSOC will assess progress made towards the Millennium Development Goals, and also the implementation of the other goals and targets agreed at the major UN conferences and summits over the past 15 years.

Functional Commissions

- UN Commission for Social Development
- UN Commission on Human Rights (UNCHR) :

Disbanded 2006, replaced by the United Nations Human Rights Council (UNHRC), a subsidiary organ of the General Assembly.

- Commission on Narcotic Drugs
- Commission on Crime Prevention and Criminal Justice
- Commission on Science and Technology for Development (CSTD)
- Commission on Sustainable Development (CSD)
- UN Commission on the Status of Women (UN CSW)
- Commission on Population and Development
- UN Statistical Commission
- United Nations Forum on Forests

Regional Commissions

- United Nations Economic Commission for Europe (ECE)
- United Nations Economic Commission for Africa (ECA)
- United Nations Economic Commission for Latin America and the Caribbean (ECLAC)
- United Nations Economic and Social Commission for Asia and the Pacific (ESCAP)
- United Nations Economic and Social Commission for Western Asia (ESCWA)

Specialized Agencies

The Specialized Agencies are autonomous organizations working with the United Nations and each other, inter alia through the coordinating machinery of the Economic and Social Council.

- ILO - International Labour Organization

- FAO - Food and Agriculture Organization
- UNESCO - United Nations Educational, Scientific and Cultural Organization
- WHO - World Health Organization
- World Bank Group
    - o IBRD - International Bank for Reconstruction and Development
    - o IDA - International Development Association
    - o IFC - International Finance Corporation
    - o MIGA - Multilateral Investment Guarantee Agency
    - o ICSID - International Centre for Settlement of Investment Disputes
- IMF - International Monetary Fund
- ICAO - International Civil Aviation Organization
- IMO - International Maritime Organization
- ITU - International Telecommunication Union
- UPU - Universal Postal Union
- WMO - World Meteorological Organization
- WIPO - World Intellectual Property Organization
- IFAD - International Fund for Agricultural Development
- UNICEF - United Nations Children Fund
- UNIDO - United Nations Industrial Development Organization
- UNDP - United Nations Development Programme
- IRO - International Refugee Organization (ceased to exist in 1952)
- INCB - International Narcotics Control Board

Other Entities

- Permanent Forum on Indigenous Issues (PFII)
- Sessional and Standing Committees Expert, ad hoc and related bodies
- UNICEF-United Nations International Children's Emergency Fund

Background

The Economic and Social Council (ECOSOC) serves as the central forum for discussing international economic and social issues, and for formulating policy recommendations addressed to Member States and the United Nations system. It is responsible for promoting higher standards of living, full employment, and economic and social progress; identifying solutions to international economic, social and health problems; facilitating international cultural and educational cooperation; and encouraging universal respect for human rights and fundamental freedoms. It has the power to make or initiate studies and reports on these issues. It also has the power to assist the preparations and organization of major international conferences in the economic and social and related fields and to facilitate a coordinated follow-up to these conferences. With its broad mandate the Council's purview extends to over 70 per cent of the human and financial resources of the entire UN system.

The ECOSOC was established under the United Nations Charter as the principal organ to coordinate economic, social, and related work of the 14 UN specialized agencies, 10 functional commissions and five regional commissions. The Council also receives reports from 11 UN funds and programmes.

In the Millennium Declaration, Heads of State and Government decided to further strengthen the Economic and Social Council, building on its recent achievements, to help it fulfill the role ascribed to it in the UN Charter. In carrying out its mandate, ECOSOC consults with academics, business sector representatives and more than 2,100 registered non-governmental organizations . The Council holds a four-week substantive session each July, alternating between New York and Geneva , and it is organized under the High-level Segment, Coordination Segment, Operational Activities Segment, Humanitarian Affairs Segment and the General Segment. At the High-level segment, national cabinet ministers and chiefs of international agencies and other high officials discuss in detail a selected theme of global significance. A Ministerial declaration is generally adopted on the theme of the High-level Segment, which will provide policy guidance and recommendations for action.

Policy Leadership

ECOSOC has taken a lead role in key policy areas in recent years:

- The 1999 High-level segment issued a "Manifesto on Poverty" which, in many respects, anticipated the formulation of the Millennium Development Goals that were approved at the UN Millennium Summit in New York .
- The Ministerial Declaration of the High-level Segment in 2000 proposed specific actions to address the digital divide, leading directly to the formation in 2001 of the ICT [Information and Communication Technologies] Task Force .
- The consideration of African development at the 2001

High-level Segment resulted in the first formal international endorsement of the New Partnership for Africa 's Development (NEPAD).

- The 2002 High-level Segment adopted an innovative resolution on the contribution of human resources, in particular in the area of health and education, to development.
- The 2003 High-level Segment on the "promotion of an integrated approach to rural development in developing countries for poverty eradication and sustainable development" led to a renewed attention of the issue and the launch of a related initiative on Madagascar.
- The 2004 High-level Segment focused on Least Developed Countries and resources mobilization and an enabling environment for poverty eradication. The High-level Dialogue of the Council helped to highlight the specific problems of LDCs. It also led to the launch of a rural initiative in Benin .
- The 2005 High-level Segment, together with the coordination segment, constituted a major input to the 2005 high-level review by the General Assembly of the progress made in the implementation of the United Nations Millennium Declaration, including the internationally agreed development goals and the global partnership required for their achievement.
- The 2006 High-level Segment focused on the issues of full and productive employment and decent work, and its impact on the sustainable development. The ECOSOC Ministerial Declaration of 2006 identified a number of concrete steps for further implementation of the 2005 World Summit to make full and productive employment and decent work a central objective of national and international policies. The Council also held informal

discussions on the Annual Ministerial Review and the Development Cooperation Forum, two new functions that ECOSOC will undertake starting 2007.

Outside of the substantive sessions, ECOSOC initiated in 1998 a tradition of meeting each April with finance ministers heading key committees of the Bretton Woods institutions. These consultations initiated inter-institutional cooperation that paved the way for the success of the International Conference on Financing for Development , held in March 2002 in Monterrey , Mexico and adopted the Monterrey Consensus . At that conference, ECOSOC was assigned a primary role in monitoring and assessing follow-up to the Monterrey Consensus. These ECOSOC meetings have been considered important for deepening the dialogue between the United Nations and the Bretton Woods institutions, and for strengthening their partnership for achieving the development goals agreed at the global conferences of the nineties. Participation in the meetings has broadened since the initial meeting in 1998. In addition to the chairperson of the Development Committee of the World Bank and the chairperson of the International Monetary and Financial Committee of the International Monetary Fund, the General Council of the World Trade Organization and the Trade and Development Board of UNCTAD are now also participating in the meeting.

United Nations Economic Commission for Europe

The United Nations Economic Commission for Europe (UNECE or ECE) was established in 1947 to encourage economic cooperation among its member States. It is one of five regional commissions under the administrative direction of United Nations headquarters. It has 56 member States, and reports to the UN Economic and Social Council (ECOSOC). As well as countries in Europe, it includes the United States of America, Canada, Israel and the Central Asian republics. The UNECE secretariat headquarters is in Geneva, Switzerland and has a budget in the region of $50 million.

Member States

The 56 member countries are:

- Albania
- Andorra
- Armenia
- Austria
- Azerbaijan
- Belarus
- Belgium
- Bosnia and Herzegovina
- Bulgaria
- Canada
- Croatia
- Cyprus
- Czech Republic
- Denmark
- Estonia
- Finland
- Former Yugoslav Republic of Macedonia
- France
- Georgia
- Germany
- Greece

- Hungary
- Iceland
- Ireland
- Israel
- Italy
- Kazakhstan
- Kyrgyzstan
- Latvia
- Liechtenstein
- Lithuania
- Luxembourg
- Malta
- Moldova
- Monaco
- Montenegro
- Netherlands
- Norway
- Poland
- Portugal
- Romania
- Russia
- San Marino
- Serbia
- Slovakia
- Slovenia
- Spain
- Sweden
- Switzerland
- Tajikistan

- Turkey
- Turkmenistan
- Ukraine
- United Kingdom
- United States
- Uzbekistan

Note: 15 of the UNECE's 56 member countries are recipients of Official Development Assistance.

United Nations Economic Commission for Africa

The United Nations Economic Commission for Africa (UNECA or ECA) was established in 1958 by the United Nations Economic and Social Council to encourage economic cooperation among its member states (the nations of the African continent) following a recommendation of the United Nations General Assembly. It is one of five regional commissions. The ECA has 53 member states corresponding to the 53 member states of the United Nations that lie within the continent of Africa.

UNECA Member States

Programme: The Commission's work is structured into seven programme divisions:

- African Centre for Statistics
- Food Security & Sustainable Development
- Gender and Social development
- ICT and Science & Technology
- NEPAD & Regional Integration
- Trade, Finance & Economic Development
- Governance & Public Administration

Locations

- Addis Ababa, Ethiopia (headquarters)
- Yaoundé, Cameroon (Central African subregional headquarters)
- Kigali, Rwanda (East African subregional headquarters)
- Tangier, Morocco (North African subregional headquarters)
- Lusaka, Zambia (Southern African subregional headquarters)
- Niamey, Niger (West African subregional headquarters)

United Nations Economic Commission for Latin America and the Caribbean

The United Nations Economic Commission for Latin America and the Caribbean (UNECLAC or ECLAC) was established in 1948 (then as the UN Economic Commission for Latin America, or UNECLA) to encourage economic cooperation among its member states. In 1984, a resolution was passed to include the countries of the Caribbean in the name. It is one of five regional commissions under the administrative direction of United Nations headquarters.

The ECLAC has 44 member States and eight non-independent territories in the Caribbean, and reports to the UN Economic and Social Council (ECOSOC). As well as countries in Latin America and the Caribbean, it includes Canada, France, Germany, the Netherlands, Portugal, Spain, Italy, the United Kingdom, the United States, Japan and South Korea.

Member States

- Antigua and Barbuda

- Argentina
- Bahamas
- Barbados
- Belize
- Bolivia
- Brazil
- Canada
- Chile
- Colombia
- Costa Rica
- Cuba
- Dominica
- Dominican Republic
- Ecuador
- El Salvador
- France
- Germany
- Grenada
- Guatemala
- Guyana
- Haiti
- Honduras
- Italy
- Jamaica
- Japan (27 July 2006)
- Mexico
- Netherlands
- Nicaragua
- Panama

- Paraguay
- Peru
- Portugal
- Saint Kitts and Nevis
- Saint Lucia
- Saint Vincent and the Grenadines
- South Korea (5 June 2007)
- Spain
- Suriname
- Trinidad and Tobago
- United Kingdom of Great Britain and Northern Ireland
- United States of America
- Uruguay
- Venezuela

Associate Members

- Anguilla
- Aruba
- British Virgin Islands
- Montserrat
- Netherlands Antilles
- Puerto Rico
- Turks and Caicos Islands (24 March 2006)
- United States Virgin Islands

Locations

- Santiago, Chile (headquarters)
- Mexico City, Mexico (Central American subregional headquarters)

- Port of Spain, Trinidad and Tobago (Caribbean subregional headquarters)
- Buenos Aires, Argentina (country office)
- Brasília, Brazil (country office)
- Montevideo, Uruguay (country office)
- Bogotá, Colombia (country office)
- Washington, DC, United States of America (liaison office)

Executive Secretaries of ECLAC

Name	Country	Served
Gustavo Martínez Cabañas	Mexico	December 1948 – April 1950
Raúl Prebisch	Argentina	May 1950 – July 1963
José Antonio Mayobre	Venezuela	August 1963 – December 1966
Carlos Quintana	Mexico	January 1967 – March 1972
Enrique V. Iglesias	Uruguay	April 1972 – February 1985
Norberto González	Argentina	March 1985 – December 1987
Gert Rosenthal	Guatemala	January 1988 – December 1997
José Antonio Ocampo	Colombia	January 1998 – August 2003
José Luis Machinea	Argentina	December 2003 to June 2008
Alicia Bárcena	México	July 2008 to present

United Nations Economic and Social Commission for Asia and the Pacific

The Economic and Social Commission for Asia and the Pacific (UNESCAP or ESCAP), located in Bangkok, Thailand, is the regional arm of the United Nations Secretariat for the Asian and Pacific region. It was established in 1947 (then as the UN Economic Commission for Asia and the Far East) to encourage economic cooperation among its member states.

The name was changed to the current in 1974. It is one of five regional commissions under the administrative direction of United Nations headquarters. The ESCAP has 53 member States and nine Associate members, and reports to the UN Economic and Social Council (ECOSOC). As well as countries in Asia and the Pacific, it includes France, the Netherlands, the United Kingdom and the United States. The ESCAP is headed by Executive Secretary Noeleen Heyzer of Singapore. Ms. Heyzer is the first woman to head ESCAP, which is the biggest of the UN's five regional commissions, both in terms of population served and area covered.

Fifty-three countries are members of ESCAP, and there are nine countries which are associate members. ESCAP's regional focus is managing globalization through programs in environmentally sustainable development, trade, and human rights.

Member States

- Afghanistan
- Armenia
- Australia
- Azerbaijan
- Bangladesh
- Bhutan
- Brunei Darussalam
- Cambodia
- China, People's Republic of

- Fiji
- France
- Georgia
- India
- Indonesia
- Islamic Republic of Iran
- Japan
- Kazakhstan
- Kiribati
- Democratic People's Republic of Korea (North Korea)
- Republic of Korea (South Korea)
- Kyrgyzstan
- Lao People's Democratic Republic
- Malaysia
- Maldives
- Marshall Islands
- Federated States of Micronesia
- Mongolia
- Myanmar
- Nauru
- Nepal
- Netherlands
- New Zealand
- Pakistan
- Palau
- Papua New Guinea
- Philippines
- Russian Federation

- Samoa
- Singapore
- Solomon Islands
- Sri Lanka
- Tajikistan
- Thailand
- Timor-Leste
- Tonga
- Turkey
- Turkmenistan
- Tuvalu
- United Kingdom of Great Britain and Northern Ireland
- United States of America
- Uzbekistan
- Vanuatu
- Vietnam

Associate Members

- American Samoa
- Cook Islands
- French Polynesia
- Guam
- Hong Kong, China
- Macau, China
- New Caledonia
- Niue
- Northern Mariana Islands

United Nations Economic and Social Commission for Western Asia

The United Nations Economic and Social Commission for Western Asia (UN-ESCWA), headquartered in Beirut, Lebanon, is one of the five regional commissions under the administrative direction of the United Nations Economic and Social Council. UN-ESCWA promotes economic and social development of Western Asia through regional and subregional cooperation and integration. It devises, promotes, and executes development assistance activities and projects in tune with the needs and priorities of the region of Western Asia. UN-ESCWA coordinates its activities with those of the major departments/offices of the United Nations at Headquarters and of specialized agencies and inter-governmental organizations, such as the League of Arab States, the Gulf Cooperation Council and the Organization of the Islamic Conference, with a view to avoid duplication and ensure complementarity, synergy and exchange of information. ESCWA has 13 member States,and reports to the UN Economic and Social Council (ECOSOC).

The United Nations Economic and Social Commission for Western Asia (UN-ESCWA or ESCWA) was first established in 1973 as the UN Economic Commission for Western Asia (UN-ECWA). It was established by Economic and Social Council resolution 1818 (LV)and was the successor to United Nations Economic and Social Office in Beirut (UNESOB). The organization's name was changed from Economic Commission for Western Asia (ECWA) to Economic and Social Commission for Western Asia (ESCWA) in 1985.

Member States

- Bahrain

- Egypt
- Iraq
- Jordan
- Kuwait
- Lebanon
- Oman
- Palestine
- Qatar
- Saudi Arabia
- Syria
- United Arab Emirates
- Yemen

Locations

UN-ESCWA headquarters is located in Downtown Beirut, Lebanon, near the Grand-Serail - the headquarter of Lebanese Prime Minister - and the Parliament.

Funding

The administrative budget of UN-ESCWA is funded from the financial resources of the United Nations, the major portion of which comes from the contributions of member States. Detailed expenditures are allocated to various sections for pre-determined purposes.

Furthermore, UN-ESCWA receives additional financial resources from outside the regular budget, which are used to implement specific projects in accordance with agreements reached with governmental and non-governmental donors. The amount of these resources varies from one period of time to another, depending on numerous considerations and circumstances.

6

United Nations Secretariat

The United Nations Secretariat is one of the principal organs of the United Nations and it is headed by the United Nations Secretary-General, assisted by a staff of international civil servants worldwide. It provides studies, information, and facilities needed by United Nations bodies for their meetings. It also carries out tasks as directed by the UN Security Council, the UN General Assembly, the UN Economic and Social Council, and other U.N. bodies. The United Nations Charter provides that the staff be chosen by application of the "highest standards of efficiency, competence, and integrity," with due regard for the importance of recruiting on a wide geographical basis.

The Charter provides that the staff shall not seek or receive instructions from any authority other than the UN. Each UN member country is enjoined to respect the international character of the Secretariat and not seek to influence its staff. The Secretary-General alone is responsible for staff selection.

The Secretary-General's duties include helping resolve international disputes, administering peacekeeping operations, organizing international conferences, gathering information on the implementation of Security Council decisions, and consulting with member governments regarding various initiatives. Key Secretariat offices in this area include the Office of the Coordinator of Humanitarian Affairs and the Department of Peacekeeping Operations.

The Secretary-General may bring to the attention of the Security Council any matter that, in his or her opinion, may threaten international peace and security.

On 21 March 2005, Secretary-General Kofi Annan proposed several reforms for the Secretariat. He announced his intentions to appoint a Scientific Adviser, create a peacebuilding support office, establish a cabinet-style decision-making mechanism, and strengthen the mediation function. He also asked the General Assembly to appropriate funds for a one-time staff buyout; to work with him in revising budgetary and human resources rules; to grant the Secretary-General more managerial authority and flexibility; to strengthen the Office of Internal Oversight Services; and "to review all mandates older than five years to see whether the activities concerned are still genuinely needed or whether the resources assigned to them can be reallocated in response to new and emerging challenges".

Organization

- United Nations Office of the Secretary-General
- United Nations Office of Internal Oversight Services
- United Nations Office of Legal Affairs

- United Nations Department of Political Affairs
- United Nations Department for Disarmament Affairs
- United Nations Department of Peacekeeping Operations
- United Nations Office for the Coordination of Humanitarian Affairs
- United Nations Department of Economic and Social Affairs
- United Nations Department of General Assembly and Conference Management
- United Nations Department of Public Information
- United Nations Department of Management
- United Nations Office of the Iraq Programme
- United Nations Office of the United Nations Security Coordinator
- United Nations Office of the High Representative for the Least Developed Countries, Landlocked Developing Countries and Small Island Developing States
- United Nations Office on Drugs and Crime
- United Nations Office at Geneva
- United Nations Office at Vienna
- United Nations Office at Nairobi

Secretaries-General

- Trygve Lie, Norway (1945-1953)
- Dag Hammarskjöld, Sweden (1953-1961)
- U Thant, Burma (1961-1971)

- Kurt Waldheim, Austria (1972-1981)
- Javier Pérez de Cuéllar, Peru (1982-1991)
- Boutros Boutros-Ghali, Egypt (1992-1996)
- Kofi Annan, Ghana (1997-2006)
- Ban Ki-moon, South Korea (2007-*incumbent*)

7

NGO Participation At The United Nations

NGOs and Global Policy-Making

Organizations like Oxfam, Greenpeace, Amnesty International and thousands of others serve the public on a national and international scale. Known variously as "private voluntary organizations," "civil society organizations," and "citizen associations," they are increasingly called "NGOs," an acronym that stands for "non-governmental organizations."

The United Nations system uses this term to distinguish representatives of these agencies from those of governments. While many NGOs dislike the term, it has come into wide use, because the UN system is the main focus of international rule-making and policy formulation in the fields where most NGOs operate.

Charitable and community organizations, separate from the state, have existed in many historical settings, but NGOs are primarily a modern phenomenon. With the extension of citizenship rights in Europe and the Americas in the eighteenth and nineteenth centuries, people founded increasing numbers of these organizations, as instruments to meet community needs, defend interests or promote new policies.

The French writer Alexis de Toqueville emphasized the importance of what he called "political associations" as institutions of democracy, uniquely numerous and influential in the United States at the time of his famous visit in 1831. New legal rules for private corporations, emerging at this same time, provided modern juridical authority for the organizations and increased their defenses against state interference.

The anti-slavery movement, founded in England in the late 18th century, gave rise to many such organizations and eventually led to the World Anti-Slavery Convention (1840), a milestone gathering to coordinate the work of citizen organizations on an international basis. The World Alliance of YMCAs was founded soon after, in 1855, and the International Committee for the Red Cross came into being in 1863. During the nineteenth century, independent associations of this kind addressed many issues, including women's rights, the condition of the poor, alcohol abuse and municipal reform. Trade unions emerged as a leading force in the NGO movement later in the century.

Today, NGOs address every conceivable issue and they operate in virtually every part of the globe. Though international NGO activity has grown steadily, most NGOs operate within a single country and frequently they function within a purely local setting. Some, such as legal assistance organizations, mainly provide services. Some such as chambers of commerce, concern themselves with narrowly-defined interests. And some, such as neighborhood associations, promote civic beautification or community improvement. But many important NGOs, such as those working for human rights and social justice, campaign for broad ideals. At the international level, thousands of organizations are active. According to one estimate, some 25,000 now qualify as international NGOs (with programs and affiliates in a number of countries) – up from less than 400 a century ago. Amnesty International, for example, has more than a million members and it has affiliates or networks in over 90 countries and territories. Its London-based International Secretariat has a staff of over 300 which carries out research, coordinates worldwide lobbying and maintains an impressive presence at many international conferences and institutions.

Political scientists often refer to NGOs as "pressure groups" or "lobby groups," but this concept does not do justice to these organizations and their broad public influence. In the 1980s, the term "civil society" came into fashion, but it proved too broad and amorphous. For this reason, a cross-disciplinary specialty emerged in the 1990s focusing on NGOs and their role in society. Scholars working in this area have noted that NGOs can command great legitimacy, sometimes more than national authorities. An opinion poll in Germany, for example, found that considerably more respondents said they trusted the NGO Greenpeace than those that expressed trust in the German Federal government. NGOs create "public goods," needed by citizens, that are not ordinarily created in the for-profit marketplace. Economists sometimes refer to NGOs and the broader, non-profit part of the economy as the "Third Sector," to distinguish it from government and private business. In some large countries, this sector accounts for millions of jobs and billions of dollars of economic activity.

NGOs are often seen as synonymous with non-profits, but a distinction between the two is useful. Non-profits include a very wide range of organizations, including museums, universities, and hospitals, that focus on services and rarely (if ever) engage in advocacy. By contrast, NGOs always have an important advocacy mission.

In the field of international relations, scholars now speak of NGOs as "non-state actors" (a category that can also include transnational corporations). This term suggests NGOs' emerging influence in the international policy arena where previously only states played a significant role. Though NGOs have few formal powers over international decision-making, they have many accomplishments to their credit.

In recent years, they have successfully promoted new environmental agreements, greatly strengthened women's rights, and won important arms control and disarmament measures. NGOs have also improved the rights and well-being of children, the disabled, the poor and indigenous peoples. Some analysts believe that these successes resulted from increasing globalization and the pressure of ordinary citizens to control and regulate the world beyond the nation state.

NGO work on the environment led to the adoption of the Montreal Protocol on Substances Depleting the Ozone Layer in 1987. The International Campaign to Ban Land Mines, an NGO coalition, was prime mover in the Mine Ban

Treaty of 1997. The Coalition for an International Criminal Court was indispensable to the adoption of the 1998 Treaty of Rome and another NGO mobilization forced governments to abandon secret negotiations for the Multilateral Agreement on Investments in 1998. In the late 1990s, the NGO Working Group on the Security Council emerged as an important interlocutor of the UN's most powerful body, while the Jubilee 2000 Campaign changed thinking and policy on poor countries' debt. At the same time, an increasingly influential international NGO campaign demanded more just economic policies from the World Trade Organization, the International Monetary Fund and the World Bank. These recent NGO victories have often been due to effective use of the internet, enabling rapid mobilization of global constituencies.

NGOs operate with many different methods and goals. Some act alone while others work in coalitions. Some organize noisy protests and demonstrations while others prefer sober education or quiet diplomacy. Some "name and shame" those in power who abuse citizen rights, while others work closely with the authorities. Some simplify the issues for broad public campaigns, while others produce detailed studies to inform policy makers.

NGO action can be analyzed on three different levels: micro-policy, macro-policy and norm-setting. Some NGO campaigns combine all three. For example, the World Court Project, a network of NGOs opposed to nuclear weapons, successfully brought a landmark case to the World Court in 1996 on the legality of nuclear weapons. Getting the Court to accept the case was a victory in the arena of micro-policy, but the larger campaign goal included macro-policy (changing governments' strategic reliance on nuclear weapons) and norm-setting (persuading the public that nuclear weapons are immoral and a threat to real security).

Governments and international organizations at times find NGOs a nuisance or even threatening to their interests. But officials nonetheless look to NGOs for innovative ideas and information. Officials also grudgingly recognize that consultation with (and support from) NGOs gives their public decisions more credibility. Former Secretary General Boutros Ghali affirmed that NGOs "are an indispensable part of the legitimacy" of the United Nations, while his successor Kofi Annan has said that NGOs are "the conscience of humanity."

NGOs are very diverse and by no means all are equally laudable. In addition to the great organizations dealing with human rights, environmental protection and humanitarian assistance, there are NGOs representing industry associations like soap and chemicals, narrowly zealous religious organizations and advocates of obscure causes like Esperanto and space colonization. While some NGOs are fiercely independent, others are known as the creatures of governments, businesses or even criminal interests. Some have hundreds of thousands of members around the world while others speak for only a handful of people. Some have large central secretariats and some are very decentralized. With such diversity, generalizations about NGOs can be difficult.

Recently, the number of NGOs has been growing rapidly. Thousands of NGOs have sprung up in such diverse countries as France, Bangladesh, the Philippines and Chile. Many observers see these trends as signs of increasing pluralism and democracy, because authoritarian and paternalistic governments have either outlawed independent NGOs or confronted them with severe administrative hurdles and harassment. Large numbers of NGOs certainly help to reflect a complex and diverse social reality and represent a rich variety of citizens' needs and concerns that governments on their own could scarcely identify or accommodate.

As NGOs take an increasingly important role in political life, some critics are concerned that NGOs speak in many different and conflicting voices, that can fragment and weaken political action. Often, there are many competing NGOs in the same policy field and their mutual contest for influence can undercut political effectiveness. Many respected NGOs work hard to overcome this narrowness by operating in close partnership with others. Some NGOs themselves specialize in coalition-building. Interaction, for instance, serves as the umbrella for dozens of humanitarian organizations in the United States.

Even the most democratic governments subject NGOs to some type of control, such as registration and financial oversight. International organizations like the UN require officially-accredited NGOs to pass through a review process to determine which are legitimate partners. Thanks partly to these controls and to the ethos of public service in the NGO community, NGOs are not often accused of corruption, breaches of the law, gross failure to live up to their mandate or other serious abuses. Compared with the frequent scandals of corruption and abuse of authority by officials of nation states, NGOs appear as relatively virtuous.

Nonethelsss, some accuse NGOs of being structurally

undemocratic and unaccountable. Elected government officials often defend themselves against NGO criticism by pointing out that NGO leaders are not elected. Though it is true that NGO leaders do not stand for election, they are held accountable by boards of directors, membership bodies, and other constituencies. They also must win voluntary financial support each year from members and donors and cannot rely on legally-enforced taxation as governments do.

Financing

Large international NGOs may have operational budgets in the tens of millions of dollars, though most NGO budgets are considerably smaller. Compared to corporations and governments that count their annual revenue in multiple billions, even the largest NGO budgets are very small indeed. NGOs are usually financed by a combination of sources. Traditionally, membership dues have provided the main source, but today NGOs tap many other sources including grants or contracts from governments and international institutions, fees for services, profits from sales of goods, and funding from private foundations, corporations and wealthy individuals.

Increasingly, relief and development NGOs like CARE and Oxfam receive large grants from governments' international assistance programs. In the 1990s, the UN High Commissioner for Refugees expressed alarm that governments were increasingly channeling funds for humanitarian assistance to their own national NGOs rather than to multilateral agencies. The agencies were losing their capacity to coordinate relief in large scale emergencies, as dozens of NGOs appeared on the scene. By 1994, European

Union funding of NGOs had risen to about $1 billion. According to UN staffer Antonio Donini, public grants represented 1.5% of NGO income in 1970 and 35% in 1988. Such grants probably accounted for more than 40% of NGO income by the end of the century. This trend inevitably exposes NGOs to pressure from governments and limits their capacity to act independently.

When NGOs take money from businesses, big foundations and rich individuals, such hefty grants can likewise create relations of influence and potentially lead NGOs away from their mandate to serve the broader public. Increasingly also, NGOs sell products or services, just like a private company. The American Association of Retired Persons (AARP) is an extreme example of this tendency. In 1996 it had $3.8 billion in gross revenue for supplemental health insurance and nine mutual funds with $13.7 billion in assets. To many observers, this looks more like a financial services company than an NGO. Thousands of other hard-pressed NGOs worldwide have taken the business path — selling credit cards, internet services, travel tours and key rings, while charging for services they once provided free.

Diplomatic Role

Though NGOs have long operated internationally, their role in the sphere of official diplomacy was relatively restricted until after World War II. NGOs won their right to a voice at the United Nations by heavy lobbying during the wartime negotiations (1943-45). Their rights were eventually guaranteed by Article 71 of the UN Charter and affirmed by many subsequent decisions. By 2000, about 2,500 NGOs had consultative status with the UN and many thousands more had official arrangements with other organs in the UN system and other intergovernmental bodies.

The Earth Summit in Rio in 1992 set the pace for intense NGO participation in world conferences, with 17,000 NGO representatives participating in the NGO parallel forum and 1,400 directly involved in the intergovernmental negotiations. NGOs helped make the conference a success, claimed an important place in the conference declaration and played a key role in developing post-conference institutions, like the Commission on Sustainable Development.

Three years later, the Fourth World Conference on Women in September 1995 attracted an astonishing 35,000 NGO representatives to Beijing to the parallel forum and 2,600 to the intergovernmental negotiations.

NGOs have been most effective when they work together in coalitions, pooling their resources and coordinating their lobbying efforts. There are important NGO networks on the environment and on international economic policy that allow NGOs to coordinate their actions in many countries and at international conferences and negotiations. Third World Network, based in Malaysia, is an especially active example that addresses a very broad range of policy issues. There are national networks like the Philippine-based Freedom from Debt Coalition and the German NGO Network on Environment and Development. And there are regional networks like ARENA, the Asian Regional Exchange for New Initiatives, or the Continental Network of Indigenous Women of the Americas, or AFRODAD, the African Debt and Development Network. In 1995, an international consultation of NGO networks concluded that: "Business and government are organized at the international level. There is a growing need to articulate countervailing visions . . . In the long run, we have to invent the infrastructure so citizens can participate effectively in the democratic management of the global system. Over the next decade, NGOs and their networks are one of the important precursors of an accountable global civil society."

As discussions continue about democracy and accountability in global decision-making, it becomes increasingly clear that NGOs have a vital role to play. Globalization has created both cross-border issues that NGOs address and cross-border communities of interest that NGOs represent. National governments cannot do either task as effectively or as legitimately. In the globalizing world of the twenty-first century, NGOs will have a growing international calling.

Submission to the President of the General Assembly by: Eurostep, Friedrich Ebert Stiftung, Global Policy Forum, North-South Institute, Social Watch, Third World Institute, WEDO, World Federalist Movement- Institute for Global Policy

NGOs contribute valuable information and ideas, advocate effectively for positive change, provide essential operational capacity in emergencies and development efforts, and generally increase the accountability and legitimacy of the global governance process. The United Nations must strengthen and deepen its relations with NGOs in order to create a stronger, more effective and more legitimate organization. In reply to the request by the General Assembly's President for comments and input on UN/NGO relations the following points are emphasized as a way to strengthen NGO participation at the UN:

(1) *Do No Harm* : New proposals for reform of the UN should not reduce existing rights, responsibilities and forms of NGO access and participation. All UN agencies should recognize the value of cooperation with NGOs at consultative, deliberative and implementing levels of UN policies and actions.

(2) *Human Rights Council*: The new Human Rights Council must honor NGO rights stipulated in ECOSOC Resolution 1996/31 from the Commission, as provided by the GA Resolution A/RES/60/251. Likewise, NGOs should be fully involved in discussions leading to the adoption of new rules and procedures for the Human Rights Council. The transfer from the Commission to the Council must not weaken or eliminate any of the current NGO rights and privileges with the Commission.

(3) *Peacebuilding Commission*: In contrast to the strong language on NGO rights in the Human Rights Council resolution, the resolution on the Peacebuilding Commission (A/RES/60/180) only contains vague provisions for NGO consultations. Clear means must be developed for NGOs to interact and, as appropriate, participate in deliberations of the Peacebuilding Commission.

(4) *Hearings Do Not Replace Global Conferences & PrepComs:* Complementary to other forms of participation, hearings can serve to present the experiences and positions of NGOs to governments and the UN. While hearings may have a value in promoting NGO input in addressing specific issues, they should

complement rather than replace more extensive and effective forms of NGO participation. The model of the global conferences of the 1990s, with a series of preparatory committee meetings in the run-up, provides a much better means for NGO contribution and contact with delegations in the negotiating process, as well as discussion between governments and NGOs at the national level. The consultative and open process provided by the Prep Coms ensures dedicated participation by both governments, international organizations and NGOs and inspires far greater ownership of the outcome by all parties.

The UN should return to this method for all substantial decision-making processes. The "multi-stakeholder dialogues," now gaining wide currency, have not proven to be effective mechanisms. They rarely encourage real dialogue and frequently are poorly attended by member states.

(5) *Headquarters Renovation & the UN Physical Plant*: NGOs must be assured full access during the lengthy process of Headquarters renovation and full consultations should take place on this matter. NGOs should have an opportunity to give input into the UN Capital Master Plan to insure that NGO needs are met in the design. In the meantime, earphones in public galleries should immediately be made fully workable to enable NGO access to the debates.

(6) *NGLS*: NGLS must continue to enjoy independent status within the UN system. Its annual budget of approximately $1 million must be fully supported. The UN regular budget should bear a substantial proportion (at least half) of the budget requirement and other UN

agencies, programs and funds should pick up the remainder.

(7) *An NGO Portfolio in the Executive Office of the Secretary General:* The Secretary General should name a high-level person in his office to assume the role of facilitating relations with NGOs. No one in the Executive Office has had this responsibility since the departure of ASG Gillian Martin Sorensen in 2003.

(8) *GA "Hearings" on NGO Access and Participation:* To promote intergovernmental action on NGO access and participation issues, the GA President should hold "hearings" so as to clarify issues and develop a clear path forward. The hearings must be open and inclusive, with the maximum participation of NGOs from the South. There should be a possibility to submit written statements for those unable to travel.

(9) *NGO Role with ECOSOC & the UNGA*: Plans for reform of ECOSOC should take into account new ways for NGOs to consult with the Council, as well as re-enforcing existing arrangements. The General Assembly should also consider additional ways to formalize consultative arrangements with NGOs, which at present are primarily informal and ad hoc. A formal role for NGOs should be arranged on a more permanent basis, in particular for the standing committees. Use of existing ECOSOC and DPI procedures should continue to be the basis for NGO status.

(10) *Consult with NGOs Worldwide:* The UN should redouble its efforts to consult with NGOs worldwide, especially in developing countries. A fund to assist southern NGOs' participation in meetings and conferences should receive solid support from donor countries.

8

International Court of Justice

Location of the International Court of Justice in The Hague The International Court of Justice (known colloquially as the World Court or ICJ; French: Cour internationale de Justice) is the primary judicial organ of the United Nations. It is based in the Peace Palace in The Hague, Netherlands, sharing the building with the Hague Academy of International Law, a private centre for the study of international law. Several of the Court's current judges are either alumni or former faculty members of the Academy.

Established in 1945 by the UN Charter, the Court began work in 1946 as the successor to the Permanent Court of International Justice. The Statute of the International Court of Justice, similar to that of its predecessor, is the main constitutional document constituting and regulating the Court. The ICJ should not be confused with the International Criminal Court, which also potentially has "global" jurisdiction.

The Court's workload is characterised by a wide range of judicial activity. Its main functions are to settle legal disputes submitted to it by member states and to give advisory opinions on legal questions submitted to it by duly authorized international organs, agencies and the UN General Assembly. The ICJ has dealt with relatively few cases in its history, but there has clearly been an increased willingness to use the Court since the 1980s, especially among developing countries. The United States withdrew from compulsory jurisdiction in 1986, and so accepts the court's jurisdiction only on a case-to-case basis. Chapter XIV of the United Nations Charter authorizes the UN Security Council to enforce World Court rulings, but such enforcement is subject to the veto power of the five permanent members of the Council. Presently there are twelve cases on the World Court's docket.

Composition

Public hearing at the ICJ.The ICJ is composed of 15 judges elected to nine year terms by the UN General Assembly and the UN Security Council from a list of persons nominated by the national groups in the Permanent Court of Arbitration. The election process is set out in Articles 4–12 of the ICJ statute. Judges serve for nine year terms and may be re-elected for up to two further terms. Elections take place every three years, with one-third of the judges retiring (and possibly standing for re-election) each time, in order to ensure continuity within the court.

Should a judge die in office, the practice has generally been to elect a judge of the same nationality to complete the term. No two may be nationals of the same country. According to Article 9, the membership of the Court is supposed to represent the main forms of civilization and of the principal legal systems of the world. Essentially, this has meant common law, civil law and socialist law (now post-communist law). Since the 1960s four of the five permanent members of the Security Council (France, Russia, the United Kingdom, and the United States) have always had a judge on the Court. The exception was China (the Republic of China until 1971, the People's Republic of China from 1971 onwards), which did not have a judge on the Court from 1967–1985, because it did not put forward a candidate. The rule on a geopolitical composition of the bench exists despite the fact that there is no provision for it in the Statute of the ICJ.

Article 2 of the Statute provides that all judges should be "elected regardless of their nationality among persons of high moral character", who are either qualified for the highest judicial office in their home states or known as lawyers with sufficient competence in international law. Judicial independence is dealt specifically with in Articles 16-18. Judges of the ICJ are not able to hold any other post, nor act as counsel. In practice the Members of the Court have their own interpretation of these rules. This allows them to be involved in outside arbitration and hold professional posts as long as there is no conflict of interest. A judge can be dismissed only by a unanimous vote of other members of the Court. Despite these provisions, the independence of ICJ judges has been questioned. For example, during the Nicaragua Case, the USA issued a communiqué suggesting that it could not present sensitive material to the Court because of the presence of judges from Eastern bloc states.

Judges may deliver joint judgments or give their own separate opinions. Decisions and Advisory Opinions are by majority and, in the event of an equal division, the President's vote becomes decisive. Judges may also deliver separate dissenting opinions.

Ad hoc Judges

Article 31 of the statute sets out a procedure whereby ad hoc judges sit on contentious cases before the Court. This system allows any party to a contentious case to nominate a judge of their choice (usually of their nationality), if a judge of their nationality is not already on the bench. Ad hoc judges participate fully in the case and the deliberations, along with the permanent bench. Thus, it is possible that as many as seventeen judges may sit on one case.

This system may seem strange when compared with domestic court processes, but its purpose is to encourage states to submit cases to the Court. For example, if a state knows it will have a judicial officer who can participate in deliberation and offer other judges local knowledge and an understanding of the state's perspective, that state may be more willing to submit to the Court's jurisdiction. Although this system does not sit well with the judicial nature of the body, it is usually of little practical consequence. Ad hoc judges usually (but not always) vote in favour of the state that appointed them and thus cancel each other out.

Chambers

Generally, the Court sits as full bench, but in the last fifteen years it has on occasion sat as a chamber. Articles 26-29 of the statute allow the Court to form smaller chambers, usually 3 or 5 judges, to hear cases. Two types of chambers are contemplated by Article 26: firstly, chambers for special categories of cases, and second, the formation of ad hoc chambers to hear particular disputes. In 1993 a special chamber was established, under Article 26(1) of the ICJ statute, to deal specifically with environmental matters (although this chamber has never been used).

Ad hoc chambers are more frequently convened. For example, chambers were used to hear the Gulf of Maine Case (USA v Canada). In that case, the parties made clear they would withdraw the case unless the Court appointed judges to the chamber who were acceptable to the parties. Judgments of chambers may have less authority than full Court judgments, or may diminish the proper interpretation of universal international law informed by a variety of cultural and legal perspectives. On the other hand, the use of chambers might encourage greater recourse to the Court and thus enhance international dispute resolution.

Current Composition

As of March 2007, the composition of the Court is as follows:

Name	Country	Position	Elected	Term End
Dame Rosalyn Higgins	United Kingdom	President	1995, 2000	2009
Awn Shawkat Al-Khasawneh	Jordan	Vice-President	2000	2009
Raymond Ranjeva	Madagascar	Member	1991, 2000	2009
Shi Jiuyong	China	Member	1994, 2003	2012
Abdul G. Koroma	Sierra Leone	Member	1994, 2003	2012
Gonzalo Parra Aranguren	Venezuela	Member	1996, 2000	2009
Thomas Buergenthal	United States	Member	2000, 2006	2015
Hisashi Owada	Japan	Member	2003	2012
Bruno Simma	Germany	Member	2003	2012
Peter Tomka	Slovakia	Member	2003	2012

Ronny Abraham	France	Member	2005	2014
Sir Kenneth Keith	New Zealand	Member	2006	2015
Bernardo Sepúlveda Amor	Mexico	Member	2006	2015
Mohamed Bennouna	Morocco	Member	2006	2015
Leonid Skotnikov	Russia	Member	2006	2015

Jurisdiction

As stated in Article 93 of the UN Charter, all 192 UN members are automatically parties to the Court's statute. Non-UN members may also become parties to the Court's statute under the Article 93(2) procedure.

For example, before becoming member nations, Switzerland used this procedure in 1948 to become a party; Nauru also became a party in 1988. Once a state is a party to the Court's statute, it is entitled to participate in cases before the Court. However, being a party to the statute does not automatically give the Court jurisdiction over disputes involving those parties. The issue of jurisdiction is considered in the two types of ICJ cases: contentious issues and advisory opinions.

Contentious Issues (adversarial proceedings)

In contentious cases (adversial proceedings seeking to settle a dispute), the ICJ produces a binding ruling between states that agree to submit to the ruling of the court. Only states may be parties in contentious cases. Individuals, corporations, parts of a federal state, NGOs, UN organs and self-determination groups are excluded from direct participation in cases, although the Court may receive information from public international organisations. This does not preclude non-state interests from being the subject of proceedings if one state brings the case against another. For example, a state may, in case of "diplomatic protection", bring a case on behalf of one of its nationals or corporations.

Jurisdiction is often a crucial question for the Court in contentious cases. The key principle is that the ICJ has jurisdiction only on the basis of consent. Article 36 outlines four bases on which the Court's jurisdiction may be founded.

First, 36(1) provides that parties may refer cases to the Court (jurisdiction founded on "special agreement" or "compromis"). This method is based on explicit consent rather than true compulsory jurisdiction. It is, perhaps, the most effective basis for the Court's jurisdiction because the parties concerned have a desire for the dispute to be resolved by the Court and are thus more likely to comply with the Court's judgment.

Second, 36(1) also gives the Court jurisdiction over "matters specifically provided for ... in treaties and conventions in force". Most modern treaties will contain a compromissory clause, providing for dispute resolution by the ICJ. Cases founded on compromissory clauses have not been as effective as cases founded on special agreement, since a state may have no interest in having the matter examined by the Court and may refuse to comply with a judgment. For example, during the Iran hostage crisis, Iran refused to participate in a case brought by the US based on a compromissory clause contained in the Vienna Convention on Diplomatic Relations, nor did it comply with the judgment. Since the 1970s, the use of such clauses has declined. Many modern treaties set out their own dispute resolution regime, often based on forms of arbitration.

Third, Article 36(2) allows states to make optional clause declarations accepting the Court's jurisdiction. The label "compulsory" which is sometimes placed on Article 36(2) jurisdiction is misleading since declarations by states are voluntary. Furthermore, many declarations contain reservations, such as exclusion from jurisdiction certain types of disputes ("ratione materia"). The principle of reciprocity may further limit jurisdiction. As of October 2006, sixty-seven states had a declaration in force. Of the permanent Security Council members, only the United Kingdom has a declaration. In the Court's early years, most declarations were made by industrialised countries. Since the Nicaragua Case, declarations made by developing countries have increased, reflecting a growing confidence in the Court since the 1980s. Industrialised countries however have sometimes increased exclusions or removed their declarations in recent years. Examples include the USA, as mentioned previously and Australia who modified their declaration in 2002 to exclude disputes on maritime boundaries (most likely to prevent an impending challenge from East Timor who gained their independence two months later).

Finally, 36(5) provides for jurisdiction on the basis of declarations made under the Permanent Court of International Justice's statute. Article 37 of the Statute similarly transfers jurisdiction under any compromissory clause in a treaty that gave jurisdiction to the PCIJ.

In addition, the Court may have jurisdiction on the basis of tacit consent (forum prorogatum). In the absence of clear jurisdiction under Article 36, jurisdiction will be established if the respondent accepts ICJ jurisdiction explicitly or simply pleads on the merits. The notion arose in the Corfu Channel Case (UK v Albania) (1949) in which the Court held that a letter from Albania stating that it submitted to the jurisdiction of the ICJ was sufficient to grant the court jurisdiction.

Advisory opinion

An advisory opinion is a function of the Court open only to specified United Nations bodies and agencies. On receiving a request, the Court decides which States and organizations might provide useful information and gives them an opportunity to present written or oral statements. Advisory Opinions were intended as a means by which UN agencies could seek the Court's help in deciding complex legal issues that might fall under their respective mandates. In principle, the Court's advisory opinions are only consultative in character, though they are influential and widely respected. Whilst certain instruments or regulations can provide in advance that the advisory opinion shall be specifically binding on particular agencies or states, they are inherently non-binding under the Statute of the Court. This non-binding character does not mean that advisory opinions are without legal effect, because the legal reasoning embodied in them reflects the Court's authoritative views on important issues of international law and, in arriving at them, the Court follows essentially the same rules and procedures that govern its binding judgments delivered in contentious cases submitted to it by sovereign states. An advisory opinion derives its status and authority from the fact that it is the official pronouncement of the principal judicial organ of the United Nations.

Advisory Opinions have often been controversial, either because the questions asked are controversial, or because the case was pursued as an indirect "backdoor" way of bringing what is really a contentious case before the Court. Examples of advisory opinions can be found in the section advisory opinions in the List of International Court of Justice cases article. One such well-known advisory opinion is the Nuclear Weapons Case.

The ICJ and the Security Council

Article 94 establishes the duty of all UN members to comply with decisions of the Court involving them. If parties do not comply, the issue may be taken before the Security Council for enforcement action. There are obvious problems with such a method of enforcement. If the judgment is against one of the permanent five members of the Security Council or its allies, any resolution on enforcement would then be vetoed. This occurred, for example, after the Nicaragua case, when Nicaragua brought the issue of the U.S.'s non-compliance with the Court's decision before the Security Council. Furthermore, if the Security Council refuses to enforce a judgment against any other state, there is no method of forcing the state to comply.

The relationship between the ICJ and the Security Council, and the separation of their powers, was considered by the Court in 1992 in the Pan Am case. The Court had to consider an application from Libya for the order of provisional measures to protect its rights, which, it alleged, were being infringed by the threat of economic sanctions by the United Kingdom and United States. The problem was that these sanctions had been authorised by the Security Council, which resulted with a potential conflict between the Chapter VII functions of the Security Council and the judicial function of the Court. The Court decided, by eleven votes to five, that it could not order the requested provisional measures because the rights claimed by Libya, even if legitimate under the Montreal Convention, prima facie could not be regarded as appropriate since the action was ordered by the Security Council. In accordance with Article 103 of the UN Charter, obligations under the Charter took precedence over other treaty obligations. Nevertheless the Court declared the application admissible in 1998. A decision on the merits has not been given since the parties (United Kingdom, United States and Libya) settled the case out of court in 2003.

There was a marked reluctance on the part of a majority of the Court to become involved in a dispute in such a way as to bring it potentially into conflict with the Council. The Court stated in the Nicaragua case that there is no necessary inconsistency between action by the Security Council and adjudication by the ICJ. However, where there is room for conflict, the balance appears to be in favour of the Security Council.

Should either party fail "to perform the obligations

incumbent upon it under a judgment rendered by the Court", the Security Council may be called upon to "make recommendations or decide upon measures" if the Security Council deems such actions necessary. In practice, the Court's powers have been limited by the unwillingness of the losing party to abide by the Court's ruling, and by the Security Council's unwillingness to impose consequences.

However, in theory, "so far as the parties to the case are concerned, a judgment of the Court is binding, final and without appeal," and "by signing the Charter, a State Member of the United Nations undertakes to comply with any decision of the International Court of Justice in a case to which it is a party."

For example, the United States had previously accepted the Court's compulsory jurisdiction upon its creation in 1946, but in Nicaragua v. United States withdrew its acceptance following the Court's judgment in 1984 that called on the U.S. to "cease and to refrain" from the "unlawful use of force" against the government of Nicaragua. The Court ruled (with only the American judge dissenting) that the United States was "in breach of its obligation under the Treaty of Friendship with Nicaragua not to use force against Nicaragua" and ordered the United States to pay war reparations.

Examples of contentious cases include:

- A complaint by the United States in 1980 that Iran was detaining American diplomats in Tehran in violation of international law.
- A dispute between Tunisia and Libya over the delimitation of the continental shelf between them.

- A dispute over the course of the maritime boundary dividing the U.S. and Canada in the Gulf of Maine area.

A complaint by the Federal Republic of Yugoslavia against the member states of the North Atlantic Treaty Organisation regarding their actions in the Kosovo War. This was denied on 15 December 2004 due to lack of jurisdiction, because the FRY was not a party to the ICJ statute at the time it made the application.

Generally, the Court has been most successful resolving border delineation and the use of oceans and waterways. While the Court has, in some instances, resolved claims by one State espoused on behalf of its nationals, the Court has generally refrained from hearing contentious cases that are political in nature, due in part to its lack of enforcement mechanism and its lack of compulsory jurisdiction. The Court has generally found it did not have jurisdiction to hear cases involving the use of force..

Law Applied

When deciding cases, the Court applies international law as summarised in Article 38. Article 38 of the ICJ Statute provides that in arriving at its decisions the Court shall apply international conventions, international custom, and the "general principles of law recognized by civilized nations". It may also refer to academic writing ("the teachings of the most highly qualified publicists of the various nations") and previous judicial decisions to help interpret the law, although the Court is not formally bound by its previous decisions under the doctrine of stare decisis. Article 59 makes clear that the common law notion of precedent or stare decisis does not apply to the decisions of the ICJ. The Court's decision binds only the parties to that particular controversy. Under 38(1)(d), however, the Court may consider its own previous decisions. In reality, the ICJ rarely departs from its own previous decisions and treats them as precedent in a way similar to superior courts in common law systems. Additionally, international lawyers commonly operate as though ICJ judgments had precedential value.

If the parties agree, they may also grant the Court the liberty to decide ex aequo et bono ("in justice and fairness"), granting the ICJ the freedom to make an equitable decision based on what is fair under the circumstances. This provision has not been used in the Court's history. So far the International Court of Justice has dealt with about 130 cases.

Procedure

The ICJ is vested with the power to make its own rules. Court procedure is set out in Rules of Court of the International Court of Justice 1978 (as amended on 29 September 2005).

Cases before the ICJ will follow a standard pattern. The case is lodged by the applicant who files a written memorial setting out the basis of the Court's jurisdiction and the merits of its claim. The respondent may accept the Court's jurisdiction and file its own memorial on the merits of the case.

Preliminary Objections

A respondent who does not wish to submit to the jurisdiction of the Court may raise Preliminary Objections. Any such objections must be ruled upon before the Court can address the merits of the applicant's claim. These objections must be ruled upon by the Court before it can proceed on the merits. Often a separate public hearing is held on the Preliminary Objections and the Court will render a judgment. Respondents normally file Preliminary Objections to the jurisdiction of the Court and/or the admissibility of the case. Inadmissibility refers to a range of arguments about factors the Court should take into account in deciding jurisdiction; for example, that the issue is not justiciable or that it is not a "legal disput".

In addition, objections may be made because all necessary parties are not before the Court. If the case necessarily requires the Court to rule on the rights and obligations of a state that has not consented to the Court's jurisdiction, the Court will not proceed to issue a judgment on the merits.

If the Court decides it has jurisdiction and the case is admissible, the respondent will then be required to file a Memorial addressing the merits of the applicant's claim. Once all written arguments are filed, the Court will hold a public hearing on the merits.

Once a case has been filed, any party (but usually the Applicant) may seek an order from the Court to protect the status quo pending the hearing of the case.

Such orders are known as Provisional (or Interim) Measures and are analogous to interlocutory injunctions in United States law. Article 41 of the statute allows the Court to make such orders. The Court must be satisfied to have prima facie jurisdiction to hear the merits of the case before granting provisional measures.

Applications To Intervene

In cases where a third state's interests are affected, that state may be permitted to intervene in the case, and participate as a full party. Under Article 62, a state "with an interest of a legal nature" may apply; however, it is within the Court's discretion whether or not to allow the intervention. Intervention applications are rare - the first successful application occurred in 1990.

Judgment and Remedies

Once deliberation has taken place, the Court will issue a majority opinion. Individual judges may issue separate opinions (if they agree with the outcome reached in the judgment of the court but differ in their reasoning) or dissenting opinions (if they disagree with the majority). No appeal is possible, though any party may ask for the court to clarify if there is a dispute as to the meaning or scope of the court's judgment.

The International Court has been criticised with respect to its rulings, its procedures, and its authority. As with United Nations criticisms as a whole, many of these criticisms refer more to the general authority assigned to the body by member states through its charter than to specific problems with the composition of judges or their rulings. Major criticisms include:

"Compulsory" jurisdiction is limited to cases where both parties have agreed to submit to its decision, and, as such, instances of aggression tend to be automatically escalated to and adjudicated by the Security Council.

Organizations, private enterprises, and individuals

cannot have their cases taken to the International Court, such as to appeal a national supreme court's ruling. U.N. agencies likewise cannot bring up a case except in advisory opinions (a process initiated by the court and non-binding).

Other existing international thematic courts, such as the ICC, are not under the umbrella of the International Court.

The International Court does not enjoy a full separation of powers, with permanent members of the Security Council being able to veto enforcement of even cases to which they consented in advance to be bound.

9

NGO Access At The UN

Introduction

In an era of rapid globalization, non-governmental organizations (NGOs) increasingly operate in a global policy environment. Amnesty International, Doctors Without Borders, Oxfam, Greenpeace, and many others, seek to influence the great international decisions of the day. So they need to interact with global institutions. They want to participate in the process where policies are decided. The United Nations, the main global policy body, has been unusually open to NGO input over the years.

Nation states are usually the decision-makers, but NGOs seek "access" to information and to those that make the decisions. This can mean many things. NGO representatives want physical access to the conference halls where official meetings take place, so that they can observe, interact with delegates and monitor proceedings. NGO representatives want to circulate their own documents, to speak to meetings, to have access to documents and to gain entry to informal, preparatory meetings and the like. NGOs also want access to administrative offices in the Secretariat and other agencies, and the right to be consulted in the administration's policy-formulation and policy-implementation process. In some (rare) cases, NGOs aspire to official voting status in the decision-making process itself, as is the case in the International Labour Organisation.

At the United Nations, NGOs have had some access from the beginning. But recently those rules of access have seemed outmoded and in need of change. NGO importance soared with the global conferences of the 1990s, especially the great environmental conference at Rio in 1992, with over ten thousand NGO representatives participating. Never before had NGOs been so prominent, so full of energy and ideas, and so central to the intergovernmental negotiating process. Subsequent conferences in Vienna (1993), Cairo (1994), Copenhagen (1995) and Beijing (1996) confirmed this new level of NGO dynamism and influence. The UN and its agencies also began to subcontract many services directly to NGOs — including provision of emergency relief, demining, reconstruction, governance training and more — further magnifying NGO status.

The "NGO Review" at ECOSOC: Negotiations 1993-96

After the Rio conference, NGOs called for increased rights at the United Nations. The UN Charter, in Article 71, provided for "suitable arrangements for consultation" between NGOs and the Economic and Social Council. Over the years, some major international NGOs had developed considerable access. But with changing times, NGOs wanted broader and more flexible access. Many member states agreed. So, on July 30, 1993, less than a year after the Rio conference, the Economic and Social Council decided (in resolution E/1993/80) to open intergovernmental negotiations, aimed at expanding NGO rights.

Agreement was not as easy to reach as some had hoped. On the government side, there were mixed feelings about NGOs. Many governments in Africa, Asia and Latin America found the proddings and exposés of the human rights NGOs to be annoying or even a threat to their sovereignty, while powerful governments in Europe, North America and East Asia were not particularly keen on NGOs that pressed for economic justice, disarmament and global democracy. So behind a rhetoric of enthusiasm for NGOs lurked profound disquiet. Delegations feared changes that might weaken or even eventually sweep away nation-states' monopoly of global decision-making.

On the NGO side, also, there was neither unity nor complete enthusiasm for the changes under way. Some major international NGOs, with a strong presence at the UN, worried that a flood of new, purely "national" (i.e. based in a single country) NGOs would undermine NGO legitimacy and open the way for narrowly-based and government-influenced organizations to pour into the UN. Members of the Conference of NGOs in Consultative Status with the UN, known by its acronym CONGO, tended to represent this critical viewpoint. On the other hand, thousands of new, dynamic national NGOs , many of unquestioned legitimacy and effectiveness, pressed for a widening of the admission gates and viewed the older NGOs as a privileged elite. Each perspective had a certain validity, but the divisions were real and sometimes even acrimonious.

Negotiations dragged out for a long time - almost exactly three years. Many NGOs followed the process closely and lobbied delegations intensively. Eventually, under the able chairmanship of Amb. Ahmad Kamal of Pakistan, negotiations came to fruition on July 25, 1996. In exchange for concessions allowing more unrestricted representation for human rights NGOs, governments of the South won agreement that national NGOs would enjoy enlarged rights and that the General Assembly would take up the possibility of NGO representation in "all areas of work of the UN system."

The new ECOSOC resolution governing consultative status (E\1996\31) was paired with an ECOSOC decision (E\1996\297) that called on the General Assembly to explore wider arrangements. The two documents were adopted simultaneously. In spite of misgivings by some, there was widespread relief and enthusiasm among NGOs that a long and difficult process was over. Many thought - or at least hoped - that a new era for NGOs was dawning.

Short-Lived Euphoria cn General Assembly Access (September-December 1996)

Following the summer ECOSOC victory, many NGOs hoped to press forward for expanded rights. In particular, they hoped that they could obtain consultative rights with the General Assembly where informally NGOs had long enjoyed quite considerable access. On this project, the two wings of the recently-divided NGO movement were united, though there were some disagreements among NGO groupings over strategy for the new campaign. NGO were especially optimistic because they saw an ally in the incoming president of the General Assembly, Amb. Razali Ismail of

Malaysia, who took office in September 1996. Razali was a longtime representative of unusual dynamism and intelligence, who had strong ties to many NGOs, particularly those in the environmental field. He opened his presidency with an unprecedented lunch with NGOs at the Malaysian mission and his presidential office was always open to NGO input. He assured his NGO friends that he would do his best to promote a decision for wider NGO access at the earliest possible moment.

Under the leadership of the World Federalist Movement and CONGO, the access issue gained considerable headway in the early fall. NGO strategists hoped that the General Assembly would adopt a quick resolution, giving NGOs consultative status with the Assembly, including access to the main committees, subsidiary bodies and special sessions. After that, it was hoped that more difficult and controversial negotiations would get under way regarding still wider NGO rights. But with few exceptions, member states were cool towards further progress. The issue soon bogged down in procedural questions: how would the General Assembly even take up the question? Would it be in a Working Group or some other forum? And would the discussions be in private or in an open forum to which NGOs would have access?

In an effort to get the issue moving and to assuage NGO concerns about government secrecy, President Razali asked Ambassador Kamal to convene "hearings" - some of which were open to NGOs and some for delegations only. The hearings allowed many NGOs to make comments and express their hopes - and for member states to comment as well. The most concrete proposal came from the World

Federalists, who circulated a draft text on access to the General Assembly. Finally, in late 1996, faced by governmental opposition to more NGO-friendly arrangements, President Razali created a special Sub-Group of the General Assembly Working Group on the Reform of the UN System. Kamal, a candidate favored by NGOs, agreed to serve as the chair. NGOs were assured that they would have periodic, though not necessarily regular, access.

The Kamal Sub-Group (January-July 1997)

Under the chairmanship of Kamal, the Sub-Group held dozens of meetings, from January to July 1997. In a few cases, the meetings were open to NGOs. Kamal brought to bear all his diplomatic skill and his considerable knowledge of the issue, but to no avail. In spite of active cajoling from Razali and in spite of serioius efforts of a few pro-NGO delegations, the group could not even reach accord on the most basic matter - its own mandate. A number of Southern states argued for a very broad mandate, while the US and the Europeans insisted on a narrow mandate. The standoff seemed to serve the interest of most delegations. By summer, the fruitless negotiations collapsed.

In late 1996 and early 1997, a clash between the Secretariat and NGOs signalled that the Secretariat was not as NGO-friendly as the Secretary General's statements had led some to believe. Caught in a financial crisis, the UN had reduced its printing of documents and instead offered government delegations access to digital texts stored in its Optical Disk Sytem (ODS). At the same time, the UN was rapidly expanding its site on the world wide web. When NGOs asked for open access to the ODS system, the

Secretariat responded with an offer of access — but, for a fee of $1,125 per computer station per year, payable in advance. NGOs rejected the proposal, pointing out that governments increasingly make their documents freely available and noting that this decision would be especially harmful for poor, Southern-based NGOs. The NGOs called for immedicate free and open access, arguing that the web site, however welcome, was insufficient to their needs.

By coincidence, Amb. Kamal of Pakistan was also Chair of the intergovernmental body with special responsibility for this question - the Technical Sub-Group of the Working Group on Informatics of ECOSOC. NGOs sought to enlist his support in their cause, but discovered that he and his committee did not have sufficient influence over the powerful decision-makers in the Secretariat (particularly, it seems, the office of Under Secretary General Joseph Connor) to change the decision. UN budget managers saw a pay-as-you-go approach to NGOs as a symbol of their market-driven approach to reform.

Finally, on April 25, 1997, a group of twelve major NGOs presented a long and carefully-argued memo to the Secretary General asking for free ODS access. But the SG turned the issue over to lower officials and the NGO group never received any substantive response. Privately, Secretariat officials argued that funds were scarce (though they never said what the new service would cost) and they advised that the decision would not be reversed. In spite of the rhetoric of "partnership," the Secretariat never consulted NGOs about their information needs or even asked for their opinions as "consumers" of this new service.

The US Vetoes Global Conferences (Spring 1997)

Secretary-General Kofi Annan was under intense pressure from the United States, which demanded various policy changes at the UN as conditions for paying its regular dues and mounting arrears. As the UN's financial crisis deepened, UN leadership felt it had little choice but to make concessions to US policymakers, including the conservative majority in the US Congress. Among other things, Congress demanded that the UN hold no further global conferences, claiming that these were a waste of time and money. But these conferences were a popular and important means of NGO access. Because they brought together NGOs and press from the whole world, many observers considered the conferences the UN's most open and democratic forum. When the Secretary General announced his new reform "package" in the spring of 1997 he bowed to US pressure and said that he would oppose any further conferences. This came as a serious blow to NGO status at the UN.

The US Proposals and the Canada-Netherlands Initiative (Summer-Fall 1997)

In the summer of 1997, at ECOSOC meetings in Geneva, the United States introduced a draft resolution (E/1997/L.51), proposing some extension of NGO rights to the General Assembly. But the initiative offered too little and it satisfied no one, including NGOs. After several drafts, it died from lack of broader support.

By the fall of 1997, the issue appeared to be seriously bogged down and no NGO had the capacity to follow-up and push it forward. Thanks to a few friendly governments, notably Canada and the Netherlands, there were informal negotiations on a draft text dated December 9, 1997 that was a possible basis for NGO access to the GA. After a brief flurry of meetings, including meetings between NGOs and delegations, it became clear that the proposal did not have the necessary backing. Instead, the General Assembly adopted a decision (A/52/L.71) calling for a study by the Secretary General on NGO access. This, NGOs hoped, could be the basis for future action.

Incidents and Rumors (1998)

At the UN, a movement to roll back NGO rights gained force. The flashpoint was the meeting of the Commission on Human Rights in Geneva in March, 1998. Several incidents incited government ire, especially delegations of the South. The Transnational Radical Party, a political party with NGO status, accredited a large number of unaffililiated persons to the CHR - as many as seventy according to some accounts. A number of these were from Cuban emmigré groups that sharply criticized the Cuban government. The Cuban delegation responded indignantly with a proposal to limit the NGO accreditation process, by imposing a numerical limit per organization and by requiring accreditation on an annual basis only. A Cuban draft resolution began to circulate in Geneva and it was immediately apparent that it would severely damage the legitimate activities of many major NGOs.

A second incident at the CHR involved a person accredited by the FIDH - the International Federation of Human Rights Leagues. The Algerian ambassador was talking to an Algerian accredited by FIDH when two other Algerians came up and hostilely accosted the diplomat. The ambassador accused the FIDH representative of complicity in the incident, though UN security later absolved this person.

A chance encounter at UN headquarters in Geneva, also during the Commission, set off the most serious storm of all. The Indian delegate, Arundhai Ghose, spotted a person with an NGO pass who he identified as Anup Chetia, leader of an Indian sepratist group, the United Liberation Front of Assam. This group had recently taken responsibility for the kidnapping of Ghose's nephew. Outraged that such "criminals" should be allowed into the UN precincts, Ghose began a personal campaign to restrict NGOs' access and especially their physical proximity to delegates. In August, the New York Times picked up the story — a sure sign that official favor was turning against NGOs..

Then, on September 21, during the opening day of the General Debate at the General Assembly, an Iranian dissident was dragged by security guards from the gallery after causing an incident in the General Assembly chamber while the Iranian president was speaking. This person allegedly carried accreditation from the International Council of Women.

News of these incidents and a number of others made its way around the diplomatic grapevine, leading many delegations to harden their position towards NGOs and to fear that greater NGO access might lead to more nasty encounters, embarrassment and even possibly physical danger to delegates. NGOs responded by insisting that they should not be punished as a group for the alleged misdeeds of a handful. NGO leaders also pointed out that delegations were blaming organizations without a fair process for review of allegations. Some also said that an open and democratic process must accomodate a certain amount of disruption as a necessary accompanyment of free speech and protest. Surely, they insisted, the UN must adopt new approaches as it ceases to be an exclusive venue for diplomats and becomes a place where the hurly-burly of society increasingly intrudes.

Second thoughts about NGOs were not limited to delegations from the South. Rumors circulated of restrictive proposals being floated by major Northern delegations as well. According to well-informed sources, the United Kingdom delegation was privately proposing a "code of conduct" for NGOs, while the United States was suggesting that if NGOs did not submit their quadrennial reports on time they should be immediately stripped of their accreditation. A sign of the times, a number of influential pundits and publications began to reflect on a "lack of accountability" of NGOs. The influential *New York Times* ran an article that underscored these "problems" with NGOs and bracketed them with emerging mercenary companies, seeing them both as irresponsible "non-state actors," undermining governments whose "traditional functions they usurp." These developments shocked the NGO community and showed how difficult further progress was likely to be.

The Committee on NGOs and the Lobby Campaign (May-June 1998)

In May-June, 1998, the Committee on NGOs of ECOSOC (a 19-member intergovernmental body that oversees the accreditation and regulation of NGOs) held its regularly-scheduled meetings at UN headquarters in New York. One of the items on its agenda was the Cuban resolution, calling for a number of serious restrictions on NGO access. A few dozen major NGOs organized to oppose this measure. CONGO came forward with a lengthy statement and a group of human rights NGOs issued a joint statement as well. They argued that after the important progress achieved in 1996, governments would be mistaken now to retreat and to restrict NGO access.

The NGOs lobbied delegations and closely followed the meetings of the Committee. In the end, the Cubans substantially re-drafted their resolution and then decided to take it off the table. But the Cubans and their allies informed NGOs that the resolution would almost certainly be re-introduced at the Committee's meeting in December.

The Secretary General's Report (July 1998)

On July 10, 1998, the long-awaited report of the Secretary General on NGO access was finally released. Though many months had passed since the General Assembly had mandated the report, NGOs were unhappy that the office of Assistant Secretary General Gillian Sorensen had written it with virtually no NGO consultation. Not surprisingly, the report was weak and bland from an NGO point of view. On the positive side, it affirmed the importance of NGOs to the UN system and contained a useful compendium of Secretariat and UN System offices' practice in the field of NGO relations, including information about operational partnerships in relief efforts and other activities.

The report had many shortcomings, though. It offered little information about the practice of intergovernmental bodies like the GA Main Committees and not enough about the Global Conferences. It said virtually nothing about the question of NGO access to the General Assembly or any other kinds of enlarged access. While noting the sharply-increased numbers of accredited NGOs, it made no effort to assess the actual numbers of NGOs active at UN headquarters. Delegations' concerns about NGOs and security also passed without comment.

NGOs were deeply disappointed that the Secretary General had opted for caution and not taken a more vigorous initiative, in line with his own rhetoric. It was obvious that negative member state pressures — North and South alike — had substantially influenced the end result. The challenge facing NGOs was now clearer than ever.

An Inauspicious Moment (September-December 1998)

The 53rd Session of the UN opened inauspiciously. The Non-Aligned Movement at its meeting in South Africa had just issued a communique containing bad news for NGOs. Buried in the lenthy NAM statement, dated September 2, was a brief paragraph bluntly opposing expanded NGO access to the General Assembly, affirming that ECOSOC was the appropriate framework for NGO relations with the UN.

There soon followed a sharp conflict between NGOs and the Secretariat over heightened security during the General Debate, a two-week period beginning in late September when the President of the United States and many other heads of state and government address the General Assembly. UN security closed the most commonly-used NGO entrance, required NGOs to pass through a special metal detector, and subjected NGOs to unprecedented document searches. NGOs protested loudly. Soon the Chief of Security offered apologies for the document searches and officials assured NGOs that security would again be relaxed at the end of the General Debate (which it was). But security arrangements never returned to the previous norms. The Delegates' Lounge, a key meeting place, remained officially closed to NGOs until the end of the GA session in December and the NGO metal detectors stayed in place. NGOs had reason to fear a new era of restrictions and hostility.

These fears seemed confirmed when the General Assembly's Third Committee shut out NGO human rights representatives in early November from its five-year review of the Vienna Conference on Human Rights. Once again, NGOs organized on an emergency basis. And again, they won a partial victory when Human Rights High Commissioner Mary Robinson convened a special meeting to hear NGO views.

NGOs were also troubled by a rumor that the UN would begin to impose a fee for access to its important web site on international treaties, long available for free and a crucial research tool for many NGOs.

Canada's Helping Hand, the US Bombshell and Developments in ECOSOC (December 1998)

As the General Assembly considered the Secretary General's report on NGO access, NGO status seemed uncertain at best. But thanks to a timely initiative by Canada, the GA finally passed a Decision (A/53/L.68) on December 17, 1998 that asked the Secretary General to submit a second and broader report that would incorporate the views of governments, specialized agencies, observers, intergovernmental organizations and NGOs. This gave NGOs the opportunity for substantial input and it allowed time to press for a more progressive and forward-looking report in 1999.

The United State delegation dropped a bombshell on NGOs in early December by introducing a motion in the Fifth (Budget) Committee that would charge NGOs for all "costs," such as documents, use of meeting rooms, even library access. In a recently-issued report, the United Nations had estimated that such NGO costs represented 3.2% of the Conference Services budget, or some $400,000 per year to the organization. The fact that the United States, with unpaid dues of $1.3 billion, wanted to squeeze hard-pressed NGOs was greeted with outrage by the NGO community and by many member states as well. The resolution, made suddenly and secretly — and apparently against the wishes of many in the US Mission itself — was soon withdrawn. But the US substituted a motion asking the Secretariat to provide further and more detailed information on the cost of NGOs. The issue remained threateningly alive and the text of the US proposal remained a closely-held secret that no delegation would risk revealing to NGO friends.

The Cuban proposal came up again in the intergovernmental Committee on NGOs, meeting in early December. Government delegations friendly to NGOs persuaded the Committee to meet with NGO representatives. A meeting then took place on December 11. NGOs were surprised to discover that a list of alleged security problems had been circulating among committee members. And NGOs listened as some delegations complained about "unfortunate incidents," "disorderly" NGOs and "unmanageable" numbers. But on the whole the meeting was friendly. The Committee seemed ready to engage in a dialogue with NGOs and to postpone further consideration of the Cuba proposal and other restrictive measures.

The Committee meeting nonetheless demonstrated the breadth of negative ideas that NGOs confront. While the Cubans and other G-77 delegates continued to urge the need for numerical and other restrictions, the United States delegate reaffirmed the need for a "code of conduct" for NGOs, as a "means for NGOs and states to understand one another better."

At the very end of the Committee's meetings, in the final hour on the afternoon of December 18, the Chairman sought to get hasty approval for his summary of the meeting with NGOs and, stapled to the back, behind another document, a draft on "Rights and Responsibilities" of NGOs that had never been discussed. Luckily, in spite of the Chairman's efforts, the Committee refused to give its approval. Again, a negative step was just barely averted.

On a somewhat more positive note, CONGO celebrated its fiftieth anniversary on December 3, with a major meeting at headquarters, addressed by UN luminaries, delegates and NGO leaders. Congratulation was the order of the day, as speakers reviewed progress over a half century. The very next day, December 4, Assistant Secretary General Gillian Sorensen held a meeting with NGO leaders, in an unusually broad effort to consult and to invite input into the new report mandated by the pending Canadian resolution. At the time, it seemed that the Secretariat was responding to the need for new forms of consultation and partnership. But this was to prove a sad illusion.

Storms in Early 1999

In mid-February, the prestigious Stanley Foundation organized a conference on the subject of NGO access to the UN. About two dozen participants gathered in Arden House, the Harriman estate located north of New York City, for a long weekend of debate and discussion. Present were some important delegates, some key figures from the Secretariat, and a number of NGO leaders, though Assistant Secretary General Sorensen was not in attendance. For a weekend the participants talked together, took meals together, and pondered the future for NGOs. At the end, there emerged a positive conclusion that cooperation and partnership were necessary, even though the path forward would at times be rocky.

Not long after the Arden House conference, on February 25-26, CONGO held a board meeting at which members expressed serious concern about the new relations between the UN and private business. Members also discussed strained relations with the Secretariat and especially problematic relations with Assistant Secretary General Sorensen. Eventually, the board adopted a resolution on these issues and requested a meeting with Secretary General Annan to discuss them. But when CONGO president Afaf Mahfouz wrote to the SG requesting a meeting, he did not respond directly, instead forwarding the matter to ASG Sorensen.

Meanwhile, conscious of the need to provide input to the second report of the Secretary General on NGO access, a number of NGOs met privately to discuss initiatives and draft declarations. CONGO announced that it was preparing a text, and Global Policy Forum circulated a draft as well. NGOs wondered what was their best strategy, how should they frame their "input" and what issues should be raised. The Secretariat memorandum called for "comments" on the previous report, limited to four pages in length. But some NGO leaders felt that a more proactive approach and greater length would be required.

At UN offices in Geneva, Kurdish protest demonstrators broke into the premises and occupied offices in late February. The Geneva police, unable to control the situation, called in the Swiss army. The army ringed the Palais des Nations with barbed wire and patrolled the area with soldiers and heavy weapons, turning the UN into an armed camp. NGOs, along with UN staff and delegates, were subject to metal detectors and close searches. Protests on the Kosovo crisis a few weeks later would further intensify the atmosphere of security threat, having an inevitable effect on security thinking in New York.

On March 3, at a meeting of the Commission on the Status of Women, a Secretariat official prevented a Canadian NGO woman of Tibetan origin from speaking, in anticipation of objections from the Chinese delegation. When another NGO woman informed the plenary about what had taken place, the chair did not allow any further NGO speakers for the remainder of the session. A number of NGOs protested vigorously at this access setback, based on a clear principle of censorship.

On March 2, ASG Sorensen called in about a dozen NGO leaders in New York for further consultations. Discussions mainly focused on input to the Secretary General's report and plans for the Millenium Assembly and Forum. At another

NGO meeting organized by Ms. Sorensen on March 31, Chief Michael McCann of the UN Security Department spoke about security problems and the need for broad new restrictions. NGOs repeatedly asked McCann wheither he had evidence that NGOs are a real security threat, but he did not provide any convincing response. ASG Sorensen informed NGO representatives that whether they liked it or not, new restrictions would be put in place. She then asked NGOs to help devise a method for distribution of special tickets for access to the second floor of the conference building and asked for input in a few days' time.

On Friday, April 9, NGOs participating in the Sorensen discussions delivered a letter to the ASG expressing their firm opposition to the new rules and refusing to be implicated in the new system by helping to devise some of its minor details. A third meeting at the ASG's office on April 14th was especially tense. NGOs made it clear that they were very unhappy and that they felt they were being treated in an overbearing and unproductive manner. One senior NGO representative said gently but firmly that, in terms of conflict resolution, the Secretariat approach was a total failure. The meeting ended awkwardly and a meeting scheduled for the following week to solicit input to the Secretary General's report was inexplicably cancelled.

In a memorandum dated April 19, the Secretary General's Chef de Cabinet Iqbal Riza sent NGOs the new security regulations. Many new rules limited NGO access — by subjecting NGOs to searches, preventing NGOs from circulating in certain areas of the building and so on. Many NGOs were already aware of these regulations, but all were shocked at the blunt and completely unapologetic way in which they were issued. Further, according to reliable sources, Riza was issuing the rules in large part because of pressure from delegations, not because of security "threats" at all. Some said that the tough new approach was related to the SG's campaign to be reelected to a second term.

The Commission on Human Rights greatly influences UN policy towards NGOs. The Commission meetings, taking place from 22 March to 30 April 1999 drew a large number of NGOs, and conflicts with governments again arose. Especially problematic, an NGO called Christian Solidarity invited John Garang, the leader of a Southern Sudanese rebel group to speak to the Commission under its auspices. Garang inevitably annoyed the Sudanese government. And by speaking in the name of his rebel group, not the accredited NGO, he broke the Commission's rules and opened the way for rule-based reprisals. Many other delgations were annoyed at more ordinary NGO critics, who again pointed out abuses in countries world wide. In 1999, with Amnesty International highlighting the human rights abuses in the United States in its special annual report, even those delegations usually supportive of human rights NGOs were inclined to find fault.

Soon after the end of the Commission session, two ambassadors seen as "NGO friendly" took surprisingly negative steps. Ambassador Paolo Fulci of Italy, President of ECOSOC, and Ambassador Anne Anderson of Ireland, the Irish representative to the UN in Geneva and Chair of the Human Rights Commission, both wrote letters to the Chairman of the ECOSOC Committee on NGOs calling for steps to limit NGO access at the Commission, so as to make its deliberations more efficient and orderly. Human rights NGOs quickly obtained these texts and reacted with hurt and astonishment. Particularly annoying to the NGOs was the claim made by Amb. Anderson that 1,800 NGOs had "attended" the Commission. NGO research discovered that, while that number of passes had been approved, the number of passes actually issued was much smaller and that at any single session only a couple of hundred NGOs were typically present. Clearly, exaggeration on NGO numbers had become a standard means of expression govenment fear of excessive NGO influence.

A Contradictory Picture

The situation of NGOs at the end of the century is very contradictory, with movement both backward and forward. In many countries, under pressure from the political right, national legislatures changed laws, restraining the areas of legitimate NGO activities and restricting the tax-exempt status so vital to NGOs' funding base. Further, after a few years of rapid increases in government funding of NGOs, new rules and restrictions choked off the financial flows that many NGOs had come to depend on.

During 1996-98 at the UN there were also many NGO setbacks. In addition to the loss of global conferences and the ODS debacle, NGOs working in some fields found their access reduced, while others found that programs in their area suffered severely from the UN financial crisis. Disarmament NGOs, for example, faced a far more closed and less welcoming environment during the Conference on Disarmament than they had in the past. Environment NGOs felt that the status they had achieved at Rio was substantially eroded. Women's NGOs watched in frustration as many womens' programs at the UN took budget cuts.

But at the same time, in certain areas, NGOs continued to move ahead and set new precedents for participation in the intergovernmental process. Outside the UN system, NGOs proved their growing influence by engineering a new international treaty on the abolition of land mines (signed at an intergovernmental conference in Ottawa in December 1997) and by torpedoing negotiations towards a Multilateral Agreement on Investments (abandoned — for the time being at least — by governments in the summer and fall of 1998).

At the UN, during negotiations towards an International Criminal Court, NGOs achieved unprecedented access and influence and many observers hailed them as key to the eventual success of the negotiation process, as the treaty was adopted in Rome in July of 1998. At a more informal level, the NGO Working Group on the Security Council in New York opened up an effective channel for regular dialogue between NGOs and the Council — a step that had seemed impossible only a short time before. Even in the inner-sanctum of the intergovernmental process, NGOs were proving the importance of their presence — and were being treated by delegations as necessary and even welcome partners.

The NGO movement has many potential resources and its global grassroots base appears stronger than ever. Reinforced by the internet and woven together in networks of cooperation and joint action, the NGO community is clearly not going to be an easy target for hardliners on the government side. Furthermore, governments are far from being consistently hostile to NGOs. While inclined to keep NGOs "in their place," they are also keenly aware that NGOs are valuable partners, sources of information, links to the public, sources of ideas and analysis. In short, NGOs are annoying but indispensable. So delegations are constantly closing the door, only to open it again still wider. With the right kind of organization and mobilization, and with an enlightened approach from delegations, NGOs could well take another significant step forward on access to UN decision-making at the dawn of the new millenium.

Interacting Fruitfully with Un-Civil Society

Having worked with and documented "NGOs" for several decades, it has been interesting to note how research under headings such as: NGOs, voluntary associations, community organizations, third sector organizations, humanitarian organizations, non-profit bodies, and the like has been continually reframed. Different academic disciplines or approaches to development seem to have associated themselves with particular takes on what has only recently acquired a neutral label as "civil society". This term was seldom used a decade ago by many who choose to use it now. The blossoming of studies is associated with the transformation of the U.S.S.R. with few dating prior to 1989.

The debate amongst those influenced by the methodology and political constraints of the intergovernmental system was severely constrained by the UN terminology of "non-governmental organization" as specified in Article 71 of the Charter of the United Nations. It could even be argued that "civil society" acquired currency as a concept only with the transformation of the U.S.S.R.

With the cessation of the Cold War, the pressures from environmental groups resulted in major procedural changes with respect to acceptance of a wide range of bodies at the Rio Earth Summit in 1992. These precedents have encouraged rethinking of the whole question of how non-governmental bodies relate to the UN system and have raised many questions about how they may be better associated with official development programmes. This has become especially acute as a consequence of negative assessments of the capacity of official programmes to deliver development at the field level.

The rethinking on all sides may perhaps be distinguished in terms of the following trends:

- erosion of the distinction between "international" NGOs and national or local bodies (which may be their members) in terms of operational contact with inter-governmental bodies
- challenges to the concept of "consultative status" and the lack of effective involvement of non-western bodies
- challenges to the representativity of traditional world-wide NGOs by those perceived as being newer grass-roots social and citizens movements unencumbered by any questionable secretariats or decision-making apparatus
- academic research emphasis on community organizations
- efforts to define an international legal status for non-profit bodies, notably within the European region (Council of Europe) or within the European Union.
- dramatic media attention on (and by) "humanitarian organizations" in relation to crises in Somalia and

Bosnia that undermined the credibility of intergovernmental initiatives.

- efforts to take account of unenvisaged manifestations of collective organization characteristic of non-western cultures.

All of these have combined to promote discussion of NGO-related phenomena whilst at the same time handicapping effective discussion of "civil society", notably in the FSU. This has been exacerbated by what might be termed definitional games. Indeed it might be asked whether use of "civil society" is not part of just such a game.

Definitional Games: UNDP

It is difficult to avoid the suspicion that further exploration of civil society is bedeviled by definitional game-playing by parties with special interests they are seeking to promote. Any classification of the actors in civil society has become a political act —whether in relation to inter-organization competition for resources, academic schools of thought, or in the political dynamics surrounding non-governmental cooperation with intergovernmental bodies. This is best illustrated by the following paragraphs previously published elsewhere (but adapted for this paper).

In January 1995 the Management Development and Governance Division of the United Nations Development Programme (UNDP) published a discussion paper on Public Sector Management, Governance, and Sustainable Development. This was the result of several stages of internal and external consultation. It affirms that the "good management of human affairs by governments, through public sector organisations and in collaboration with organisations of civil society, is a sine qua non of sustainable human development." Its purpose is to define a position within governance for the development assistance efforts of UNDP as the major coordinating agency for development funding within the UN system.

This report can be seen as one UN response to other efforts to redefine the contemporary challenge of governance. The concern here is to highlight ways in which the report operates out of a framework which has been demonstrated as inadequate to the challenges of the past and is therefore likely to be inadequate to those of the future.

One way to formulate this inadequacy is as a marked ability to play what amounts to definitional games. In practice insightful analysis and laudable principles are elaborated at one point, only to be effectively reframed with a far more narrow and questionable interpretation at another. Whilst this may be good politics and good public relations, it does not invite confidence. Is it deliberate on the part of some, a manifestation of sloppy thinking, or a consequence of committee report writing? It is precisely this tendency which has alienated so many from political processes in general, and from UN processes in particular.

The report leads off with some fast conceptual foot-work. "Governance is the exercise of political power to manage a nation's affairs. Public management...is synonymous with governance." (p. xii) — implying that "management of the public" is also synonymous with governance? "Whatever the nature of society, only governments can set the rules according to which the system works and take corrective action when it fails" (p. 19).

This reflects profound ignorance of the "rules" established by religious movements (notably with respect to population non-control), by professional bodies (with respect to codes of conduct and peer pressure), by multinational corporations, and by those who engage so effectively in the illegal arms and drugs trade. The action of NGOs in Somalia, of Amnesty with respect to human rights abuses, and Greenpeace with respect to government-sanctioned environmental abuses, can be seen as a non-government "corrective action" when the system fails. It also reflects ignorance of the widely acknowledged consequences of globalization of information and decision-making outside governmental frameworks — if only with respect to movements of funds.

Later however we read that "Sound governance also calls for cooperation between governments and civil society organisations. Sound governance is not simply something that governments do by themselves" (p. 25). This is a typical example of a later statement reframing the scope of an earlier one (above). The major emphasis in the report on collaboration with "civil society" is indeed a striking and welcome breakthrough following decades of governmental arrogance. It parallels concerns expressed in other reports on governance. It also arouses the suspicion that, having recognized its limitations, and the progressive erosion of its credibility and resources, the intergovernmental system is anxious to associate itself with a system that is in a healthier state and which is seen to offer more genuine involvement of the people.

After several development decades "It is now widely accepted that many organisations in civil society are strongly committed to forms of development that give prominence to the social and economic needs of people and environmental protection." (p. 25). Consider the definitional games associated with this realization. "Such organisations are referred to collectively...as community organizations. Two broad types are identified: people's organisations and NGOs...People's organisations represent their members interests, are accountable to their members, and tend to have participatoryorganisational structures." (p. 25). This strongly suggests that NGOs have none of these characteristics in the eyes of those who favour this definition.

Elsewhere we read however that "Civil society organisations are multifarious. They differ according to their membership, their missions, forms of organisation, and levels of operation. They include religious-based organisations, cooperatives, trade unions, academic institutions, and community and youth groups" (p. 110). Elsewhere a distinction is made between "NGOs, community-based organisations, and other civil society organisations" (p. 99).

What does this imply as to UNDP understanding of NGOs? Only much later do we read that they can be very broadly defined as "nongovernment organisations involved in development, staffed by professionals and para-professionals, which provide services or products that cater to the needs of people at the grassroots" (p. 86). But we also read that "NGOs constitute a critical element of the civil society, but have probably received a greater share of the limelight than other deserving organisations, such as professional organisations and women's groups" (p. 86).

The definitional game being played here arises from a

long-established tendency of UNDP to ignore the scope of the UN-imposed definition of nongovernmental organization (under Article 71 of the Charter concerning consultative status arrangements) in favour of a definition of NGOs as organizations providing direct development aid, however this happens to be narrowly conceived by UNDP strategists at a given time. The UN definition (itself currently under review) allows for a much broader understanding of organizations relevant to "economic and social development" and includes "professional organizations and women's groups" and many other categories. The implicit UNDP definition, reinforced by many national NGOs (until very recently excluded from any relationship to the UN or to UNDP Resident Representatives, and resentful of the exclusiveness of the UN definition), is an effort to coopt national or local groups whilst undermining the international NGOs through which many of them have long been linked.

Definitional Games: UNESCO

"Foundations and similar institutions" are not included within the UNESCO definition of "nongovernmental organizations" and relationships with them are governed by separate directives. However responsibility for relationships with both NGOs and foundations is held by the same department within UNESCO.

According to UNDP figures however, the donations received by UNESCO from "NGOs" during 1993 (DP/1994/40/Add.1, 28 September 1994) amounted to $3.20 million dollars (an increase from $2.87 million in 1992), namely a total of $5.87 million for the 1992-93 biennium. For UNDP, the "NGOs" are the "foundations", since none of the UNESCO

"NGOs" actually donate funds to UNESCO.

UNESCO maintains relations with some 581 NGOs. The total contractual and subvention cost of funds distributed by UNESCO to NGOs was $3,265,300 for the 1992-93 biennium.

It would appear that in terms of funds alone, the NGOs (according to the broader UNDP definition) are far from being a cost to UNESCO, as Member States are wontto assume. Rather UNESCO effectively redistributes to "NGOs" about half of what it receives from "NGOs". In this sense NGOs as a category may be said to be a net financial contributor to UNESCO.

In the light of the new USA aid policies, favouring distribution of funds through NGOs rather than through intergovernmental bodies, it might be asked whether such foundations might come to the view that their funds could be more effectively used by transferring them funds directly to other NGOs rather than via the general funds of intergovernmental organizations.

Definitional Games: the United Nations NGO Review Process

The otherwise excellent General Review of Arrangements for Consultations with Non-Governmental Organizations by the UN Secretary-General (E/AC.70/1994/5, 26 May 1994) falls victim to confusion by making the unfortunate claim that "NGOs fall roughly into two categories. The first one is a category of organizations which by their objectives and methodology are concerned with supporting social movements and/or initiatives. The second category includes NGOs which have emerged from social movements and represent their institutionalized reality. The former category of NGO emphasizes participation and empowerment and sees its role needing to be focused on capacity-building for greater self-reliance at the community level. The latter focuses on advocacy and networking as tools to promote changes in policies and governance." (para. 12)

This simplistic categorization by the United Nations effectively excludes many scientific, educational and cultural NGOs in official relations with UNESCO, to say nothing of bodies having official relations with Specialized Agencies such as ILO, WHO or FAO — all of which may, in consequence, be recognized by ECOSOC at the present time. It is therefore not clear what role these bodies may be recognized as performing, if any, once the UN review process is completed under the influence of the NGOs privileged by the biased definitions of the review process.

The report fails to clarify what is effectively excluded from its focus and especially the basis for doing so. In stressing bodies which have an obvious relation to development, it fails to recognize the function of others that have a less obvious relation to development (which might typically include many of the cultural NGOs in relation with UNESCO).

"Civil Society" ?

In an earlier paper (Judge, 1995) the focus was on exploring methods of moving beyond the limitations of the many particular ways of discussing "civil society". It endeavoured to identify broader issues of relevance to public policy formulation in response to the challenge of "civil society" to governance as indicated by Yehezkel Dror (1995).

As implied above, one of the difficulties is that "civil society" itself is discussed through a variety of terms whose partial equivalence has not been effectively explored. These include: nongovernmental organizations (NGOs), voluntary associations, nonprofit sector, not-for-profit sector, charitable organizations, benevolent societies and third sector. Depending on who uses these terms, they may, or may not, includebodies such as labour unions, trade associations, professional societies, or legally unrecognized (and even illegal) bodies such as cartels and crime rings. In many cases it is not what a particular approach includes that is as significant as what is effectively excluded and why.

Many modern protagonists in such debates fail to recognize that the debate about the nature of NGOs and civil society has been in progress since the beginning of the century — as can be seen in the publications of the Union of International Associations in the period 1910-20. Many of the points concerning the relationship between governmental and nongovernmental organizations have been made many times over — some of them over a period of decades.

There is therefore merit in reflecting on the collective ability to process these questions in new and fruitful ways. There is a sense in which it is in the interests of many to avoid clarity and conclusion and simply to perpetuate the discussion. And there is the continuing interest of others to arrive at simplistic solutions if possible. The debate is complicated by a degree of unwillingness to recognize some weaknesses in the present arrangements.

Conceptual Omissions

It would appear that fruitful discussion is severely handicapped by a tendency to selective conceptual omission. A particular concern with regard to "civil society" is whether those mobilized behind this term are not misled by an apparent opportunity to impose a definition of the "good society" from which dubious forms of organization are excluded. Emphasis would then be placed on "voluntary associations", "charitable bodies", "citizens movements" and the like, especially when their activities are in no way controversial. By some, it would be considered inappropriate to include bodies such as professional organizations, trade associations, employers organizations, or labour unions.

An important issue here is the extent to which civil society bodies are to be understood as associated with economic activity and specifically with wealth generation, especially profit-making. Civil society can be readily, and conveniently, understood as encompassing all organized activity not associated with the major institutional systems: government and administration, education and health delivery, business and industry, security and organized religion. But this creates many difficulties.

It is therefore useful to distinguish three clusters:

Group A: what is included in over-simplistic understandings of "civil society" and which will continue to attract supporters of uncritical and uncontroversial under-standings of the "good society".

Group B: what can usefully be understood as "non-civil society", by opposition to simplistic understandings of "civil society", namely government and other establishment institutions.

Group C: what then remains to be considered as part of the social fabric, having taken account of Group A and Group B. This might usefully be understood asthe "un-civil society".

Un-civil Society

With apologies to Mahatma Gandhi, it is appropriate to reframe his classic response to the journalist who enquired, on the occasion of Gandhi's visit to the UK, what he thought of Western Civilization. Gandhi's response that "It would be a very good idea" might equally be applied to the concept of "civil society".

There are numerous features of society, to be understood as clustered into Group C, which challenge some of the polyanna-ish aspects of Group A — for they are distinctly "un-civil" and questionable from one or other perspective. And yet they are indeed characteristic of a fuller understanding of "civil society". Depending on the position taken by the Group A advocate, they will include a greater or lesser portion of the following (Group C.1):

- labour unions, professional bodies, employers organizations
- not-for-profit research institutes
- religious bodies, including ashrams, churches, religious orders
- political parties
- cooperatives and mutual societies
- foundations and waqf
- intentional communities
- heraldic and ceremonial groups

More challenging however are bodies such as the following (Group C.2):

- gangs
- paramilitary organizations
- criminal organizations (Mafia, Yakuza, Triads, etc), drug rings
- cartels
- secret societies (including the freemasons), cults
- intelligence networks
- subversive and revolutionary political groups
- terrorist groups.

The first group above are tainted by financial or ideological considerations, whilst the second tend to be characterized by the illegality of their actions or their ability to act "above" or "beyond" the law. The situation is further complicated by Group C.3, namely "front organizations" (whether for government, ideological, religious, business or criminal groups). Further complications in understanding "civil society" are introduced when groups have only a temporary or "electronic" existence — as with the 15,000 newsgroups on the Internet (Group C.4).

And of course there are the complications associated with groups more characteristic of non-western societies — and often unknown, or of little significance, to those active in defining "civil society". These include (Group C.5):

- tribal and kinship groups
- name groups (as with the Chinese)
- guru-oriented groups
- traditional secret societies

But these have their equivalent in heraldic and ceremonial groups, often of great prestige (such as the Knights of the Garter in the UK).

Policy Implications in Relation to the FSU

Following the dismemberment of the U.S.S.R. and the transformation of Eastern Europe, many policy assumptions were made with regard to the economic transformation and development of those societies.

Considerable numbers suffered in consequence — especially the vulnerable. There has been much criticism on both sides of misguided efforts to "export" Western economic models and political institutions to those countries. This has led, to the surprise of many, to the re-emergence of former leaders of communist society, together with political parties reflecting approaches distinctly unsympathetic to any western understanding of civil society.

In the process of establishing more creative relationships with Western Europe, efforts have been made to involve the FSU in the Council of Europe. To that end the participation of Russia in the pattern of European treaties has been a critical issue. Given the distinctly non-western approach to legislation and implementation characteristic of Russian society, the appropriateness of this can be usefully questioned (Judge, 1995), as is done by Russian's themselves.

Accompanying these changes, many western bodies have endeavoured to establish relationships with people and groups in the FSU and Eastern Europe. Numerous exchanges and contacts have been fruitfully organized. Many religious groups have successfully proselytized and established viable movements, for example. At the same time there has been a flowering of a wide variety of groups and movements — strange to western eyes — often inspired by charismatic personalities characteristic of FSU cultures.

Un-civil Society and Organized Crime

But most striking, with respect to any understanding of efforts to enhance any form of "civil society" in the FSU and Eastern europe, has been the overwhelming increase in the number of criminal gangs, to the degree that it has been estimated that at least 50 percent of economic actions there are influenced by organized crime. Only extreme naivety could justify exclusion of this dimension from any discussion of civil society in the FSU.

The key policy issue here is how to understand and relate to this particular manifestation of "un-civil society" — given its central function in FSU societies at this time. Several approaches may be envisaged:

Ignore: the proliferation of gangs, and organized crime, as a particular form of "voluntary association" may be ignored as a temporary aberration, namely "civil society" may be defined to exclude such forms of social organization.

This then raises the question of the relationship in practice between "civil society", narrowly defined, and its rejected shadow the "un-civil society".

By implication, some forms of voluntary association are then understood to be naturally good, and others are to be understood as naturally inappropriate. This leaves unresolved the many dubious initiatives of "good" bodies, as evidenced by the territorial disputes between major religious groups.

It also ignores the challengeraised by the levels of abuse and fraud amongst officially registered civil society organizations in the West. But above all it loses sight of the role played by "un-civil society" in socially abnormal situations. This is equivalent to the economists error in long ignoring the "informal" or "black" economies essential to the economic success and development processes of some countries.

Exterminate: emphasis may be placed on exterminating any manifestations of "un-civil society". This loses sight of the fact that often decision-makers at the highest levels are involved, whether voluntarily or because they have been "volunteered", in un-civil activity. Even in the West, weekly scandals over the past years have revealed how ministers of government are implicated in the actions of groups acting in a distinctly un-civil manner — if only to reinforce the finances of their political parties. It is unclear what lessons are to be drawn from the Italian "clean hands" campaign in the regard, especially now that there are pressures to scale down any further investigations. Eliminating the shadow of "civil society" has never proved to be as easy as many have wished.

Come to terms: ways may be sought to "come to terms" with un-civil society. Totally unacceptable at first sight, this has proved to be the only way forward for many in the FSU. Whilst politicians may promise to "root out" organized crime, they have proved to be distinctly inept in doing so.

It is salutary to reflect on the level of gang activity in

major western cities such as Los Angeles, and the level of organized crime in many western countries, including the USA. Unfortunately it is primarily through anecdotal evidence that information on how western governments have "come to terms" with organized crime in particular situations has become available. Such information is not normally part of any course on the nature of "civil society".

Reframe: the nature of "un-civil society" may be completely reframed. The above approaches neglect the possibility that alternative understandings of the relationship between "civil" and "un-civil" society may exist in cultures other than the western. It is around this point that there have been misunderstandings concerning cultures where decision-makers naturally expect some percentage of any transaction over which they have any influence (especially when they are underpaid). The whole issue of bribery and "commissions" concerning transactions in developing countries has only recently come to the fore, as with equivalent phenomena in many industrialized countries. The legitimacy of "influence peddling" is a question in all societies. At what point do the actions of lobby groups, as manifestations of civil society in the corridors of national parliaments, acquire un-civil characteristics? When do the actions of Freemasons or Opus Dei, for example, take on "un-civil" rather than "civil" character?

Creative Challenge

Just as in the case of western attempts to export economic models and institutions, there have been efforts to export western civil society institutions. This continues a trend associated with the colonialization process in developing countries — even including the export of parliamentary models. The appropriateness of such exports was seldom questioned — as with the early priority of western missionaries to supply indigenous women with brassieres.

Almost no effort has been made to detect traditional patterns of collective organization natural to FSU and associated cultures and to seek ways of enhancing them. More challenging still would be the exploration of ways to engender new forms of collective organization in harmony with the cultural patterns and values of those societies — and of greater relevance to contemporary challenges in the FSU. What forms of organizational innovation are appropriate to the FSU? How is their encouragement to be dissociated from naively enthusiastic attempts to export (or import) inappropriate western forms?

A striking example of how such a challenge has been taken up in a developing country is offered by the Swadhaya Movement, notably active along the western coast of India.

As described by Shri R K Srivastva of the Centre for the Study of Developing Societies (New Delhi): "Swadhyaya is neither a cult nor a sect; it is neither a party nor an association; it is neither messianic nor limited to a particular section of society; it is neither directed against centralising state power nor to overcoming flaws in Indian society, though such consequences may follow. Swadhyaya is both a metaphor and a movement. It is a metaphor in the sense of a vision, and a movement in terms of its orientation in social and economic spheres."

Building on qualities long articulated within the Hindu

spiritual tradition, emphasis is placed on the quality of relationship between people, especially within the context of the most impoverished villages.

This has led to a remarkable, and growing, capacity to regenerate village life. Refusing any economic assistance from either Indian government or foreign sources, unusual achievements have been made in thousands of villages, even in such physical terms as replenishing wells and managing farms. (Ironically, although present by invitation at a 1995 FAO conference on poverty alleviation, the movement found itself isolated — it was neither in search of funds (as an "aid recipient"), nor was it offering them (as a "donor"), but its experience without funding was considered irrelevant.

Metaphors of Civil Society

There is an increasing body of literature recognizing the value of metaphor in reframing issues relating to organizational and policy innovation. The point made is the need to avoid the metaphorical traps and poverty of imagination associated with seemingly obvious options.

In this light, understandings of civil society might perhaps be compared through the following set of agricultural metaphors:

Monoculture: As with unending fields of wheat, civil society bodies might be seen as stalks of wheat, virtually indistinguishable. This image might reflect views that favour the principle of citizens organizations — providing they conform to a particular approved pattern. The creation of each body can then only take place with the approval of appropriate authorities. Differences between such bodies, from the point of view of any central authority, are considered to be negligible — only their numbers are of interest. In its most severe manifestation, all such bodies would be required to conform to central policies.

Multi-crop farming: This metaphor would allow for a limited range of differenttypes of voluntary and other organizations as making up civil society. Each type would however be well-defined: wheat, oats, turnips, cabbage, apples, etc. Within each type, variations would not be easily tolerated. This would correspond to the European Commission's approach — were it to be extended from vegetables and fruits to civil society organizations.

Integrated farming: In this metaphor, the emphasis switches to the complementarity between the different types of organization in order to optimize the growth patterns of each in the interests of the whole. The farm is treated as a system, with a water and fertilizer infrastructure, in which each crop has a distinct function.

Inter-cropping: In this metaphor attention shifts from crops as a whole. The importance of juxtaposing particular plants to provide shade, protection from insects, or soil enhancement is then emphasized. The checks and balances required within civil society are rendered explicit at the level of the individual organization rather than between classes of organization.

Permaculture: In this metaphor much greater effort is made to intimately relate a wide variety of plant and animal species to enrich the pattern of checks and balances in relation to water, sunlight, and nutrient flows.

It is with such methodologies that the skills required for sustainable communities within the civil society emerge. Permaculture is noteworthy for integrating space for uncultivated, unplanned growth as a source of particular positive influences on the cultivated species.

Natural parks: In this metaphor the concern is to protect natural patterns of growth and the wild species associated with it. In the case of civil society, this would correspond to efforts to provide for traditional forms of organization (including folk culture) — and to protect them from contemporary forms. The question of cultural identity is strongly associated with this dimension of civil society.

The challenge is to minimize forms of intervention which will make such "natural" organization appear artificial. Excessive intervention, as with artificial landscaping, can make such supposedly natural forms of civil society both artificial and soulless.

Wilderness areas: In this metaphor a much greater variety of plant and animal species grow freely without outside intervention or justification — constituting a rich genetic pool. In the case of civil society, the question for any authority is to what degree a veritable jungle of organizations of every imaginable kind can be allowed to exist without requiring constant supervision and management. Such authorities may not then have the ability to control civil society, even if they wished to. This then reflects the most extreme forms of "un-civil society".

It is interesting to reflect on the policy challenges relating to civil society in the FSU and Central/Eastern

Europe in terms of these metaphors. Essentially it is a question of what forms of organization should be cultivated and how, and how does society benefit by allowing space for certain forms to grow freely.

Past errors of agriculturists and land resource managers carry many lessons for thosehoping to cultivate civil society and develop sustainable communities. More specifically there is the issue of what should be considered "weeds", how they are to be reduced, and what should be appreciated as "wild-flowers".

The above agricultural and land management metaphors also highlight the fundamental challenge of building sustainable communities, namely ensuring appropriate interaction amongst a diversity of organizations. It is civil society as a complex ecological system of organizations which needs to be explored. Simplistic approaches to this ecology may be tantamount to the destruction of cultural rainforests.

Bibliography

Antti Pentikaiinen: *Creating Global Governance - The Role of Non-Governmental Organizations in the United Nations,* Helsinki, Finnish UN Association 2000.

Aptekar, Lewis. *Street Children of Cali,* Durham, Duke University Press,1988.

Catholics for a Free Choice: *Bad Faith at the UN: drawing back the curtain on the Catholic Family and Human Rights Institute,* Washington, DC: Catholics for a Free Choice, 2001.

Gabriel, Marie Cruz: *Children of the street,* New York, Penguin Books, 1994.

Global Policy Forum: *NGOs and the United Nations,* New York, Global Policy Forum, 1999.

Harold K. Jacobson: *Networks of Interdependence: international organizations and the global political system,* New York, Knopf, 1984.

Harry J. Steiner: *Diverse Partners: non-governmental organizations in the human rights movement,* Cambridge, Harvard Law School and Human Rights Internet, 1990.

John Boli and George Thomas: *Constructing World Culture: International Nongovernmental Organizations Since 1875,* Stanford, Stanford University Press, 1999.

John Clayton Thomas: *Public Participation in Public Decision: New Skills and Strategies for Public Managers,* San Francisco, Jossey-Bass Publishers, 1995.

John Ehrenberg: *Civil Society: The Critical History of an Idea,* New York, New York University Press, 1998.

John Foster with Anita Anand: *Whose World is it Anyway? Civil Society, the United Nations and the multilateral future,* Ottawa, United Nations Association of Canada, 1999.

Jonathan A. Fox and L. David Brown: *The Struggle for Accountability: The World Bank, NGOs, and Grassroots Movements,* Cambridge, Mass.: MIT Press, 1998.

Julie Fisher: *The Road from Rio: sustainable development and the nongovernmental movement in the Third World,* Westport, Praeger, 1993.

Marcos Arruda: *NGOs and the World Bank: Is It Possible to Collaborate Critically?,* Rio de Janeiro: PACS, 1995.

Mary Anderson: *Managing Global Chaos: Sources of and Responses to International Conflict, Washington,* DC: United States Institute of Peace Press, 1996.

Paul J. Nelson: *The World Bank and NGOs: The Limits of Apolitical Development,* New York, St. Martin's Press, 1995.

Paul Wapner: *Environmental Activism and World Civic Politics, Albany,* SUNY Press, 1996.

Peter Willetts: *Pressure Groups in the Global System,* London, Francis Pinter, 1982

Thomas Carroll: *Intermediary NGOs: the supporting link in grassroots development,* West Hartford, CT: Kumarian Press, 1992.

Thomas G. Weiss & Leon Gordenker: *NGOs, the UN & Global Governance,* Boulder, Lynne Riener, 1996.

Thomas Princen and Matthias Finger: *Environmental NGOs in World Politics,* London, Routledge, 1994.

Yolanda N. Kakabadse and Sarah Burns: *Movers and Shapers: NGOs in International Affairs,* Washington DC, World Resources Institute, 1994.

Index

Index

A

N

O

P

R

◊ ◊ ◊